GLENCOE

The **American Journey**
Early Years

Reading Essentials and Note-Taking Guide
STUDENT WORKBOOK

Mc Graw Hill **Glencoe**

The *McGraw-Hill* Companies

 Glencoe

Send all inquiries to:
Glencoe/McGraw-Hill
8787 Orion Place
Columbus, OH 43240-4027

ISBN: 978-0-07-880671-1
MHID: 0-07-880671-2

Printed in the United States of America.

1 2 3 4 5 6 066 12 11 10 09 08

CONTENTS

Chapter 17 Reconstruction and the New South

To the Student

Taking good notes helps you become more successful in school. Using this book helps you remember and understand what you read. You can use this *Reading Essentials and Note-Taking Guide* to improve your test scores. Some key parts of this booklet are described below.

The Importance of Graphic Organizers

First, many graphic organizers appear in this *Reading Essentials and Note-Taking Guide*. Graphic organizers allow you to see important information in a visual way. Graphic organizers also help you understand and summarize information, as well as remember the content.

The Cornell Note-Taking System

Second, you will see that the pages in the *Reading Essentials and Note-Taking Guide* are arranged in two columns. This two-column format is based on the **Cornell Note-Taking System,** developed at Cornell University. The large column on the right side of the page contains the essential information from each section of your textbook, *The American Journey: Early Years*.

The column on the left side of the page includes a number of note-taking prompts. In this column, you will perform various activities that will help you focus on the important information in the lesson. You will use recognized reading strategies to improve your reading-for-information skills.

Vocabulary Development

Third, you will notice that vocabulary words are bolded throughout the *Reading Essentials and Note-Taking Guide*. Take special note of these words. You are more likely to be successful in school when you have vocabulary knowledge. When researchers study successful students, they find that as students acquire vocabulary knowledge, their ability to learn improves.

Writing Prompts and Note-Taking

Finally, a number of writing exercises are included in this *Reading Essentials and Note-Taking Guide*. You will see that many of the note-taking exercises ask you to practice the critical-thinking skills that good readers use. For example, good readers make connections between their lives and the text. They also *summarize* the information that is presented and *make inferences* or *draw conclusions* about the facts and ideas. At the end of each section, you will be asked to respond to two short-answer questions and one essay. The essays prompt you to use one of four writing styles: informative, descriptive, persuasive, or expository.

The information and strategies contained within the *Reading Essentials and Note-Taking Guide* will help you better understand the concepts and ideas discussed in your social studies class. They also will provide you with skills you can use throughout your life.

Chapter 1, Section 1 (Pages 6–9)
Migration to the Americas

Essential Question

How did agriculture change the lives of the early people?

Directions: As you read, complete a graphic organizer like the one below to show the effects of agriculture on the lives of the early people.

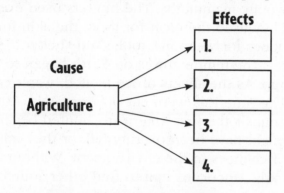

Effects

Cause

Agriculture

1.

2.

3.

4.

 **Notes** | **Read to Learn**

The Journey From Asia (pages 7–8)

Describing

Describe the way archaeologists learn about early peoples.

_____

_____

_____

The first people came to the Americas thousands of years ago. The Europeans who arrived in the late 1400s found Native Americans already living there. They wondered where the Native Americans came from. Experts in **archaeology,** the study of ancient peoples, are still trying to figure that out. They study **artifacts** of the early peoples. Artifacts include tools, weapons, baskets, and carvings. The findings of the archaeologists show that many early peoples may have come to the Americas across a strip of land that joined Asia and the Americas.

Earth has gone through several ice ages, or periods of extreme cold. During the ice ages, large sheets of ice covered much of Earth. The last Ice Age started about 100,000 years ago and ended about 12,000 years ago. The sea level was lower at this time. It exposed a land bridge connecting what are now Siberia and Alaska. Today that land bridge, called Beringia, is underwater.

The early people who came to the Americas were **nomads.** Nomads are people who move from place to place. They hunted for most of their food. During a hunt, they crossed Beringia into what is now Alaska. This crossing was a **migration.** A migration

Read to Learn

The Journey From Asia (continued)

Explaining

Complete the sentence below to explain how early people came to the Americas.

While they were

_____,

_____ crossed

_____ into

what is now _____.

is a movement of a large number of people into a new homeland. Over hundreds of years, many people traveled from Asia and spread out across the Americas.

When the first Americans arrived from Asia, they found huge animals. They used spears to hunt bison, mastodons, and woolly mammoths. The hunters used every part of the animal. They used the meat for food, the skin for clothing, and the bones for weapons, tools, and shelter.

The temperatures on Earth began to rise about 15,000 years ago. As the sheets of ice melted, water covered Beringia again. The Americas were cut off from Asia. At the same time, the animals the first Americans hunted began to die. The animals might have been overhunted, or they might have died because of changes in the environment. Without these animals to hunt, early Americans had to find other sources of food.

Settling Down (page 9)

Summarizing

How did early Americans change the way they obtained food?

_____

_____

_____

_____

Early Americans began to hunt smaller animals and fish. They gathered berries and grains. They also started to farm. In present-day Mexico, people began to raise **maize,** an early form of corn. They also raised pumpkins, beans, and squash. Farming gave the people a steady supply of food, so they did not have to move from place to place to hunt. Farming also gave people time to do other things besides finding food.

Now that the people had a steady supply of food, many of them began to settle down. Scientists have found villages that are about 5,000 years old. They use **carbon dating** to measure the amount of radioactive carbon in the artifacts from these villages. The amount of carbon in an artifact gives an estimate of the artifact's age. From these artifacts, scientists can tell that farming changed the lives of early Americans. Over time, early Americans developed common customs and beliefs. They created their own **cultures,** or ways of life.

Chapter 1, Section 1

Section Wrap-Up

Answer these questions to check your understanding of the entire section.

1. **Explaining** How were early people able to migrate to the Americas during the last Ice Age?

_____

_____

_____

2. **Determining Cause and Effect** Explain some of the factors that led to the development of new cultures in the Americas.

_____

_____

_____

In the space provided, write a magazine article describing the journey of early peoples to the Americas. Describe how they met their needs for food, clothing, and shelter. Also describe how their way of life changed when the large animals they hunted died out.

_____

_____

_____

_____

_____

_____

_____

_____

_____

_____

_____

_____

Cities and Empires

Essential Question

How did the early civilizations of Mexico and Central America develop socially, politically, and economically?

Directions: As you read, complete a graphic organizer like the one below to show how the early civilizations of Mexico and Central America developed socially, politically, and economically.

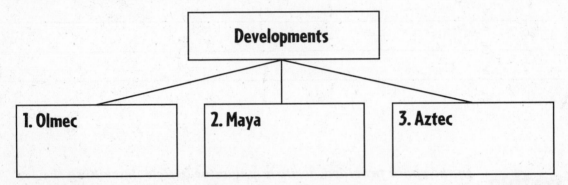

Developments

1. Olmec   2. Maya   3. Aztec

Notes

Read to Learn

The Olmec, Maya, and Aztec (pages 11–14)

Identifying

Where did the Olmec and Maya civilizations live?

1. The Olmec _____

_____

_____

2. The Maya _____

_____

_____

By the early 1500s, several **civilizations,** or highly developed societies, arose in present-day Mexico and Central America. They built large cities. They also developed complex ways of writing, counting, and keeping track of time.

The Olmec

The Olmec lived along the Gulf Coast of present-day Mexico, Guatemala, and Honduras. They lived in this area between 1500 B.C. and 300 B.C. The Olmec produced enough crops to feed thousands of people. They built large stone monuments and drainage systems, and they used pavement. The civilization ended for unknown reasons.

The Maya

The Maya lived in the rain forests of present-day Mexico, Guatemala, Honduras, and Belize. By A.D. 300, the Maya had built many large cities. Each city had at least one pyramid with a temple at the top. The Maya believed that the gods controlled

The Olmec, Maya, and Aztec (continued)

Defining

Hieroglyphics is a _____ system that uses _____ or _____ to represent things, ideas, and sounds.

everything and that only priests knew what the gods wanted. As a result, Maya civilization became a **theocracy,** a society ruled by religious leaders.

The Maya made many advances. They used their knowledge of astronomy and mathematics to develop a calendar. They also developed **hieroglyphics,** a form of writing that uses symbols or pictures to represent things, ideas, and sounds.

Maya traders carried goods from city to city on a network of roads through the jungle. They also traded by canoe along Mexico's east coast. For unknown reasons, the Maya civilization collapsed. Descendants of the Maya still live in parts of Mexico and Central America today.

The Aztec

Finding the Main Idea

Identify the main idea of each of the paragraphs about the Aztec.

1._____

_____

2._____

_____

In 1325 the Aztec settled on an island in Lake Texcoco (tehs•KOH•koh), part of present-day Mexico City. Here they built the city of Tenochtitlán (tay•NAWCH•teet•LAHN). They took soil from the bottom of the lake to make bridges to join the island and the shore. They filled parts of the lake with soil to grow crops. At one point, Tenochtitlán was the largest city in the Americas. It was also an important center of trade.

The Aztec civilization grew into a military empire. The Aztec forced the people they conquered to work as slaves. They believed that human sacrifices were necessary to please their gods, so they sacrificed thousands of prisoners of war.

The Inca (pages 14–15)

Evaluating

What do you think is the most important achievement of the Inca? Why?

_____

_____

_____

_____

The Inca Empire was the largest early American civilization. It developed in the western highlands of South America. The Inca built Cuzco (KOOS•koh), their capital city, around 1200. The Inca Empire stretched for more than 3,000 miles (4828 km). It reached from present-day Colombia to northern Argentina and Chile.

The Inca army conquered other areas. The Inca allowed the people who accepted their rule to take part in the empire's government. If the people resisted, they were treated harshly.

At its peak, the Inca ruled an empire of more than 9 million people. To control such a large empire, they built at least 10,000 miles (16,093 km) of roads. Runners carried messages to connect Cuzco to faraway parts of the empire. **Quechua** (KEH•chuh•wuh) became the language of the empire.

The Inca (continued)

Analyzing

How were the Inca able to keep records without a writing system?

_____

_____

The Inca did not have a system of writing. They kept records with knotted strings called **quipus** (KEE•poos). To farm in the mountains, the Inca cut **terraces,** or broad platforms, into the steep slopes.

The Inca believed that the emperor was a descendant of the sun god. To please this god, the Inca made gold jewelry and temple ornaments. The Inca also built cities, like Machu Picchu, just for religious ceremonies.

Section Wrap-Up

Answer these questions to check your understanding of the entire section.

1. **Analyzing** Why did the religious leaders rule the Maya?

_____

_____

2. **Comparing** How were the Aztec and Inca civilizations alike?

_____

_____

_____

Descriptive Writing

In the space provided, write a journal entry describing one of the early civilizations in Mexico, Central America, or South America, as if you had just visited there. Describe what you found particularly interesting about this civilization.

_____

_____

_____

_____

North American Peoples

Essential Question

How was the way of life of the Native Americans of North America related to their environment?

Directions: As you read, complete a graphic organizer like the one below to indicate how the way of life of Native Americans in each of the six regions was related to the environment. Give at least one example for each region.

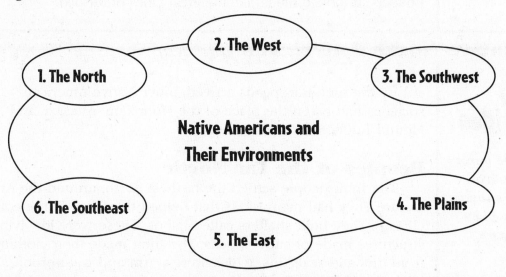

 **Notes**   **Read to Learn**

Early Native Americans *(pages 17–19)*

Comparing

Explain how the Mound Builders were similar to the Maya and Aztec.

_____

_____

_____

By the 1500s, many advanced cultures lived in North America. The Hohokam lived in present-day Arizona from about A.D. 300 to 1300. Because they lived in a dry desert, they dug irrigation channels to get river water to their crops.

The Anasazi (AH•nuh•SAH•zee) lived in the area where Utah, Colorado, Arizona, and New Mexico meet. They lived there from about A.D. 1 to 1300. They built great stone dwellings, which the Spanish explorers called **pueblos** (PWEH•blohs), or villages. The Anasazi also built dwellings in the walls of cliffs. These dwellings were easy to defend. They also protected the people from winter weather.

Several groups of people made up the large group known as the Mound Builders. The Mound Builders seem to have been influenced by the early cultures of Mexico and Central America.

Read to Learn

Early Native Americans (continued)

They built thousands of mounds of earth that looked like the pyramids of the Maya and the Aztec. Like the pyramids, some of the mounds had temples on top. The mounds are found from present-day Pennsylvania to the Mississippi River valley.

Some of the earliest Mound Builders, including the Adena, were hunters and gatherers. Later Mound Builders, like the Hopewell, were farmers and traders. Cahokia (kuh•HOH•kee•uh) in present-day Illinois was the largest settlement of Mound Builders. It looked much like the great cities of Mexico.

Other Native North Americans (pages 19–22)

Finding the Main Idea

To identify the main idea of each paragraph in this subsection, underline key words or phrases.

By the time Europeans arrived, other Native American societies had taken the place of the Hohokam, Anasazi, and Mound Builders in North America.

Peoples of the Far North

The Inuit people settled the farthest north, around the Arctic Ocean. They had many skills that helped them live in the cold climate. They built shelters called igloos. These were low-lying structures made of snow blocks. The Inuit made their clothing from furs and sealskins, which were warm and waterproof. They hunted and fished for food.

Peoples of the West Coast and the Southwest

The West Coast of North America had a mild climate and good sources of food. The peoples of the northwestern coast, like the Tlingit (TLIHNG•kuht), Haida, and Chinook, depended on the forest and the sea. They built wooden houses and fished for salmon. Salmon was also important to the peoples who lived in the plateau region between the Cascade and Rocky Mountains. The people there fished, hunted, and gathered their food.

In the dry California deserts, people gathered roots and seeds for food. Because the soil in the Great Basin region was too rocky for farming, the peoples there, such as the Ute (YOOT) and Shoshone (shuh•SHOHN), traveled in search of food. They ate small animals and gathered roots, nuts, and berries. They lived in temporary houses made from branches and reeds. In the Southwest, the Hopi, Acoma, and Zuni peoples built homes from sun-dried mud bricks called adobe. They raised crops like maize and beans. Other peoples of the Southwest, the Apache and Navajo, hunted and gathered their food.

Other Native North Americans (continued)

Analyzing

What skill helped the Native Americans of the Great Plains hunt and fight?

_____

Determining Cause and Effect

Why did the Iroquois groups form the Iroquois League?

_____

_____

_____

Peoples of the Plains

Native Americans in the Great Plains moved from place to place. They dragged their tepees, or cone-shaped skin tents, with them as they moved. They hunted antelope, deer, and buffalo and they fought on horseback, using weapons while riding.

Peoples of the East and the Southeast

The Native Americans in the woodlands of eastern North America lived in bark-covered longhouses. The Iroquois (IHR•uh•KWAH) and Cherokee had laws and set up **federations.** The federations were governments that linked different groups. The Iroquois were made up of five groups that often fought each other. In 1715 they joined together with the Tuscarora peoples to form a peace alliance called the Iroquois League. The League created a constitution. Members of the League were organized by **clans,** or groups of related families.

The Southeast was home to the Creek, Chickasaw, and Cherokee. These peoples raised crops, such as corn and squash. Their way of life was suited to their environment, which had a mild climate.

Section Wrap-Up

Answer these questions to check your understanding of the entire section.

1. **Describing** Describe the types of homes the Native Americans in North America lived in and what the homes were made of.

   _____

   _____

   _____

2. **Making Generalizations** Write a generalization about the Native American groups of North America and how they related to their environments.

   _____

   _____

Expository Writing

On a separate sheet of paper, write questions you might have asked members of one of the Native American groups in North America about how they met their needs for food, clothing, and shelter. Record a possible answer to each question.

A Changing World

Essential Question

What events and technological advances paved the way for European exploration?

Directions: As you read, complete a graphic organizer like the one below to identify the advances in technology that paved the way for European voyages of exploration.

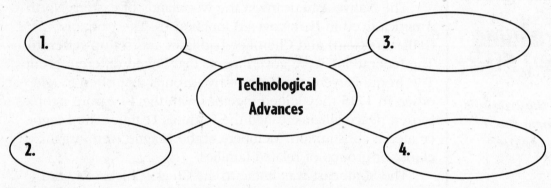

 **Notes** | **Read to Learn**

New Ideas and Nations (pages 29–30)

Defining

What was the Renaissance?

_____

_____

_____

In 1095 Europeans started the Crusades. These were expeditions to gain control of the Holy Land from the Muslims. In the Middle East, Europeans came in contact with Arab merchants who sold them spices, silks, and other goods from China and India. Interest in Asia grew after Marco Polo returned from China and described his trip.

Wealthy Europeans wanted silks and spices from the East. Merchants bought these goods from Arab traders. They sent the goods by caravan to the Mediterranean Sea and then on to Italian cities like Venice. These cities became centers of trade.

By the 1300s, trade with Asia had made Italian merchants wealthy. They became interested in science and in **classical** art and learning. Classical refers to the works of ancient Greece and Rome. This time of renewed interest in classical learning was known as the **Renaissance** (REH•nuh•SAHNTS). Over the next 200 years, it spread throughout Europe. It changed the way Europeans thought about the world.

European merchants were interested in exploration. They wanted to find a way to bypass Arab merchants and buy goods directly from the East. The start of nation-states in western

 **Notes**

Read to Learn

New Ideas and Nations (continued)

Europe added to the interest in exploration. By the 1400s, strong kings and queens had come to power in several nations. They set up national laws and armies. They also wanted to find ways to increase trade to make their countries richer.

Technology's Impact (page 31)

Listing

Name two inventions that helped sailors determine their location.

1. _____

2. _____

Advances in **technology** helped pave the way for exploration. Technology is the use of scientific knowledge for practical purposes. The introduction of the printing press in the 1450s made it possible for more people to read books and get information. Mapmakers improved the way they made maps. The maps showed lines of latitude that measured the distance north and south of the Equator.

The invention of new instruments helped sailors travel on the seas. The **astrolabe** measured the positions of stars. This helped sailors figure out their latitude while at sea. Europeans also began to use the magnetic compass, a Chinese invention. The compass helped sailors find their direction when they were far from land.

The design of ships also improved. Sailors were now able to make long ocean voyages. In the late 1400s, the Portuguese created the caravel. This ship sailed faster than other ships and could carry more goods. It could also float in shallow water. All of these inventions helped start a new time of exploration. Countries like Portugal began searching for sea routes to Asia. Portugal started by sending ships down the west coast of Africa.

African Kingdoms (pages 32–33)

Explaining

Underline the sentence that explains how Ghana became a wealthy empire.

Between A.D. 400 and 1600, several powerful kingdoms prospered in Africa. Ghana was a trading empire in West Africa. It was located between the salt mines of the Sahara and the gold mines to the south. Caravans with gold and other goods from Ghana crossed the Sahara to North Africa. There, Muslim traders loaded the caravans with salt, cloth, and other goods to take back to Ghana. Ghana grew wealthy from the taxes it collected on this trade. In 1076 people from North Africa attacked Ghana and upset its trade. Ghana then began to decline.

Another powerful kingdom, called Mali, developed in the same region. Like Ghana, it developed trade routes across the desert to North Africa. Mali was a farming area, but it grew rich from its gold mines. Mali's greatest king was Mansa Mūsā. He ruled from

 **Notes** | **Read to Learn**

African Kingdoms (continued)

Comparing

What was the religion of Mali and Songhai?

_____

1312 to 1337 and made Mali famous. In 1324 Mūsā made a grand pilgrimage to the Muslim holy city of **Makkah** (Mecca). A **pilgrimage** is a journey to a holy place. Mūsā returned to Mali with an Arab architect who built great **mosques** in Timbuktu, the Mali capital. Mosques are Muslim houses of worship. Timbuktu became an important center of Islamic learning.

In 1468 the Songhai (SAWNG•hy) people rose up against Mali rule and captured Timbuktu. Under Askìya Muhammad, the Songhai Empire became strong and traded with Europe and Asia. Askìya set up laws based on the **Quran,** the holy book of Islam. In the late 1500s, Songhai was attacked and defeated by the kingdom of Morocco.

Section Wrap-Up

Answer these questions to check your understanding of the entire section.

1. **Summarizing** How did Europeans become interested in trade with Asia?

_____

_____

2. **Drawing Conclusions** How did new technology help make exploration possible?

_____

_____

 **Descriptive Writing**

On a separate sheet of paper, write a travel article as if you are visiting the kingdom of Mali. Describe the kingdom's economy, religion, and culture.

Early Exploration

Essential Question

Why did Spain and Portugal want to find a sea route to Asia?

Directions: As you read, complete a graphic organizer like the one below to explain why Spain and Portugal wanted to find a sea route to Asia.

Portugal

1. _____
2. _____
3. _____

Spain

4. _____
5. _____
6. _____

 **Notes**

Read to Learn

Seeking New Trade Routes (pages 35–37)

Analyzing

Why was Prince Henry of Portugal important to exploration in the 1400s?

_____

_____

_____

_____

_____

Early maps showed that three continents—Europe, Asia, and Africa—were one big landmass. In the 1400s, no one knew that another big landmass—the Americas—was missing from the map. The first European nation to explore the world in the 1400s was Portugal. It did not have a port on the Mediterranean Sea, so it did not take part in the trade between Asia and Europe. Portugal's rulers wanted to find a new route to China and India. They also wanted to find a better way to get gold from West Africa.

Around 1420, Prince Henry of Portugal set up a "school of navigation" in southwestern Portugal. At the school, astronomers, geographers, and mathematicians shared their knowledge with sailors and shipbuilders. Mapmakers updated their maps as new information came in.

Portuguese ships traveled south along the coast of West Africa. The Portuguese set up trading posts where they traded for gold and ivory. King John II wanted to set up a trading empire in Asia. He believed ships could get to India and China by traveling around Africa. In 1487 Bartholomeu Dias sailed around the southernmost point of Africa. King John called this point the Cape of Good Hope. He hoped that the passage around Africa might lead to a route to India.

Seeking New Trade Routes (continued)

Identifying

Which explorer reached Brazil while trying to travel around Africa?

_____

In 1497, Vasco da Gama led the first Portuguese voyage around Africa, across the Indian Ocean and on to India. Several months after Pedro Àlvares Cabral returned home, he left on another voyage to the East. His ships swung so wide around Africa that they reached what is now Brazil. Cabral claimed this land for Portugal. He went on to India and returned with spices and other goods. The Portuguese continued their voyages to India. Soon, Lisbon, the Portuguese capital, became an important marketplace in Europe.

Columbus Crosses the Atlantic (pages 38–41)

Formulating Questions

As you read, ask yourself questions to make sure that you understand the text. Good questions begin with the words who, what, when, where, why, and how. Use one of these question words to write one question and answer about this passage in the space below.

_____

_____

_____

_____

_____

Centuries before Columbus's voyage, northern Europeans called Vikings had already reached North America. In the A.D. 800s and 900s, they visited Iceland and Greenland. Norse **sagas,** or traditional stories, tell of a Viking sailor named Leif Eriksson who explored a land west of Greenland around A.D. 1000.

By 1492, Spain was ready to look for a way to take part in the riches of the Asian trade. Christopher Columbus had a plan for reaching Asia. He decided to get there by sailing west. He was able to get the Spanish king and queen to sponsor his voyage. They did this because Columbus promised to bring Christianity to any lands he found. They also hoped that Spain would become wealthy from trade if Columbus found a way to Asia.

On August 3, 1492, Columbus set out from Spain with three ships—the *Niña,* the *Pinta,* and the *Santa María.* Columbus underestimated the size of the world and how long it should take to reach Asia. After a month at sea, his sailors began to worry. Then on October 12, 1492, they saw land. The land was part of the group of islands now known as the Bahamas. Columbus did not know it, but he had reached the Americas. He believed he had reached the East Indies, the islands off the coast of Asia. He called the people living in the Americas Indians.

Columbus made three more voyages. He explored several Caribbean islands and the coasts of Central America and South America. Eventually, it became clear that Columbus had reached a part of the world that was unknown to Europeans, Asians, and Africans.

Columbus Crosses the Atlantic (continued)

Explaining

What was the purpose of the line of demarcation?

_____

_____

_____

_____

Spain and Portugal wanted to protect their claims in the Americas. To solve the problem, Pope Alexander VI drew a **line of demarcation,** an imaginary line running down the middle of the Atlantic from the North Pole to the South Pole. Spain was allowed to control lands west of the line. Portugal controlled lands east of it. A later treaty moved the line farther west.

Other voyages followed those of Columbus. In 1502 Amerigo Vespucci determined that South America was a continent, not part of Asia. Geographers soon began calling the continent America, in Vespucci's honor. In 1513 Vasco Núñez de Balboa reached the Pacific coast of Central America. He was the first European to see the Pacific Ocean from the Americas. In 1520 Ferdinand Magellan sailed around the southernmost tip of South America. He sailed through a **strait,** or narrow sea passage, and into the Pacific Ocean. Ferdinand Magellan's crew became the first known people to **circumnavigate,** or sail around, the world.

Section Wrap-Up

Answer these questions to check your understanding of the entire section.

1. **Drawing Conclusions** Why did Christopher Columbus think he had reached the East Indies?

_____

_____

2. **Evaluating** What voyage of exploration do you think was the most important? Why?

_____

_____

**Persuasive Writing**

On a separate sheet of paper, write a letter to the Spanish monarchs as if you are Christopher Columbus. In the letter, explain why you want them to sponsor your voyage. The letter should indicate how the voyage will benefit Spain.

Spain in America

Essential Question

How did Spain's conquests affect the economic and social development of the Americas?

Directions: As you read, complete a graphic organizer like the one below to show the class system that developed in Spain's empire in the Americas.

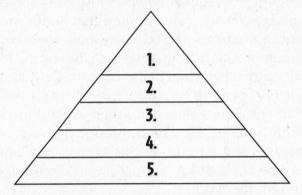

1.
2.
3.
4.
5.

 **Notes**

Read to Learn

Explorers and Conquests *(pages 43–46)*

Identifying

Which Spanish conquistadors conquered the Aztec and Inca Empires?

Aztec Empire:

_____

Inca Empire:

_____

Spanish explorers came to the Americas in search of gold and silver. These explorers were known as **conquistadors** (kahn•KEE S•tuh•DAWRS). Spanish rulers gave them the right to explore and set up settlements. The explorers agreed to give the rulers one-fifth of any treasures they found.

In 1519 Hernán Cortés landed on the east coast of present-day Mexico. He soon heard about the Aztec Empire and its capital Tenochtitlán (tay•NAWCH•teet•LAHN). The Aztec had conquered many cities in Mexico. The Aztec forced the people they conquered to give them crops and gold. Cortés formed alliances with the conquered people against the Aztec. Then he marched into the capital city with his army and Native American allies. At first, Montezuma (MAHN•tuh•ZOO•muh), the Aztec emperor, welcomed Cortés. Cortés took advantage of the friendliness and made Montezuma his prisoner. In 1521 Cortés destroyed the Aztec capital.

The conquistador Francisco Pizarro sailed down the Pacific coast of South America. He wanted the riches of the Inca Empire. This empire was located in what is now Peru. In 1532 Pizarro captured Atahualpa (AH•tah•WAHL•pah), the Inca ruler. In 1533 the Spanish executed Atahualpa. Within a few years, Pizarro controlled most of the Inca Empire.

Read to Learn

Explorers and Conquests (continued)

Determining Cause and Effect

What led Hernando de Soto and Francisco Vásquez de Coronado to explore what is now the southeastern and southwestern United States?

_____

_____

_____

_____

The Spanish conquered the Aztec and Inca quickly. They were able to do this for several reasons. First, the Spanish had weapons and animals that the Aztec and Inca had never seen before. Second, some Native Americans did not like being under Aztec rule. They helped the Spanish overthrow the Aztec. Finally, the Native Americans were not immune to European diseases. Many died from diseases like smallpox. This left them too weak to fight the Spanish invaders.

The Spanish conquistadors found gold and silver in Mexico and Peru. They hoped to find more treasures in the southeastern and southwestern parts of North America. In 1513 Juan Ponce de León explored present-day Florida. His exploration led to the first Spanish settlement in what is now the United States.

In 1536 Cabeza de Vaca (kah•BAY•sah day VAH•kah) reached Mexico. He told stories about seven cities of gold. His stories led Hernando de Soto to set out in search of these treasures. He started in what is now the southeastern United States. He crossed the Mississippi River in 1541. Francisco Vásquez de Coronado also wanted to find the seven cities. He traveled through northern Mexico and present-day Arizona and New Mexico, but did not find any gold.

Spanish Rule (pages 46–47)

Finding the Main Idea

Underline the main idea in each paragraph of this passage.

The Spanish set up three kinds of settlements in the Americas. **Pueblos,** or towns, were set up as centers of trade. **Missions** were religious communities. They usually included a small town, farmland, and a church. A presidio, or fort, was usually built near a mission.

A class system developed in Spain's empire. *Peninsulares* were at the top. They were people who were born in Spain. They owned the land and ran the local government. The class below them was the creoles. They were people who were born in the Americas to Spanish parents. Below them were the mestizos (meh•STEE•zohs). These were people with Spanish and Native American parents. Still lower were the Native Americans. At the bottom were enslaved Africans.

The Spanish gave conquistadors who settled in the Americas an **encomienda.** This was the right to demand taxes or labor from Native Americans living on the land. The system turned the Native Americans into enslaved people. Many died from lack of food and from disease. Bartolomé de Las Casas, a Spanish priest, asked the Spanish government to pass laws to protect the

Spanish Rule (continued)

Summarizing

How did the encomienda affect Native Americans?

_____

_____

_____

_____

_____

Native Americans. In 1542 the government made it illegal to enslave Native Americans.

Spanish settlers made big profits by sending crops to Spain. The main exports in the Caribbean islands were tobacco and sugarcane. To raise these crops, the Spanish set up a plantation system. A **plantation** is a large estate. At first, the Spanish used Native Americans to work the plantations. They later used enslaved Africans. Thousands of Africans from West Africa were brought to the Americas. By the late 1500s, slave labor was an important part of the economy of the colonies.

Section Wrap-Up

Answer these questions to check your understanding of the entire section.

1. **Analyzing** Why were conquistadors able to conquer the Aztec and Inca Empires so quickly?

_____

_____

2. **Determining Cause and Effect** How did slavery become an important part of the economy of the colonies?

_____

_____

 **Informative Writing**

On a separate sheet of paper, write an article explaining the kinds of settlements the Spanish set up in the Americas and the social classes that developed there.

Exploring North America

Essential Question

Why did European nations establish colonies in North America?

Directions: As you read, complete a graphic organizer like the one below to explain why European nations set up colonies in North America.

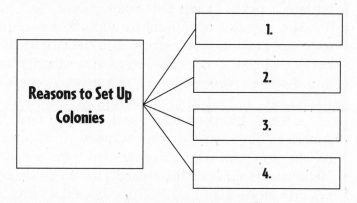

Reasons to Set Up Colonies

1.
2.
3.
4.

Notes

Read to Learn

A Divided Church (pages 49–50)

Identifying Central Issues

Why did Martin Luther break away from the Catholic Church?

_____

_____

_____

_____

_____

One of the main reasons Europeans explored and settled North America was to spread Christianity. The earliest explorers and settlers were Roman Catholics. In the 1500s, religious changes in Europe led to divisions in Christianity.

Martin Luther, a German priest, did not agree with many Church practices because they were not mentioned in the Bible. In 1517 he nailed a list of complaints against the Catholic Church on a church door. Luther and his followers soon broke away from Catholicism. Luther's protests were the start of a religious movement known as the Protestant Reformation.

Luther's ideas spread to other places. John Calvin, a French religious thinker in Switzerland, also broke away from the Catholic Church. Calvinists spread their faith to other European countries. In England, King Henry VIII also left the Catholic Church. In 1534 the English Parliament recognized the king as the head of the new Church of England.

In the Americas, Spanish and French Catholics spread their religion to Native Americans. The Spanish settled in the southwestern and southeastern parts of North America. The French settled in the northeast. Dutch and English Protestants started colonies along the Atlantic coast.

 **Notes** | **Read to Learn**

Economic Rivalry (pages 50–52)

(pages 50–52)

Defining

What was the Columbian Exchange?

_____

_____

_____

Identifying

Which countries sent explorers to find a Northwest Passage to Asia?

1. _____

2. _____

3. _____

Explaining

Why were the French interested in North America?

_____

_____

European nations also came to the Americas to gain wealth. A popular economic theory called **mercantilism** said that a nation's power is based on its wealth. European nations wanted colonies that could increase their wealth by giving them gold, silver, and raw materials. The colonies would also give the nations a place to sell European goods.

The voyages of Columbus and other explorers brought together Europe, Asia, Africa, and the Americas. The contacts between these continents led to an exchange of plants, animals, and diseases. This exchange is known as the **Columbian Exchange.** It caused great changes on all of the continents.

A treaty between Spain and Portugal had divided the Americas between the two countries. It did not allow other nations to claim land there. England, France, and the Netherlands ignored the treaty. These countries sent explorers to set up colonies and trade. They hoped to find a **Northwest Passage,** a direct water route through the Americas to Asia.

In 1497 England sent John Cabot to find the Northwest Passage. England used this exploration to claim North America. The Netherlands also sent explorers to find the Northwest Passage. Sailing for the Dutch, Henry Hudson discovered the river that now bears his name.

In 1524 France hired an Italian, Giovanni da Verrazano, to find a northern route. He explored the coast of North America from present-day Nova Scotia down to the Carolinas. In 1535 Jacques Cartier (KAR•tyay) sailed up the St. Lawrence River, hoping it would lead to the Pacific Ocean and Asia. But Cartier did not find the route to Asia.

The French did not want to build an empire in the Americas. They wanted a place to make profits from fishing and fur trading, not a place to settle. In 1608 a French fur-trading company sent Samuel de Champlain to found a settlement in what is now Quebec, Canada. The French built trading posts in other parts of Canada. There, they collected furs gathered by Native Americans and French trappers. The trappers were called **coureurs de bois** (ku•RUHR•duh•BWAH). This means "runners of the woods."

The Dutch were eager for trade. They sent a large fleet of trading ships all over the world. In 1621 the Dutch West India Company set up a colony in North America near the Hudson River. It was called New Netherland. The center of the colony was New Amsterdam, located on Manhattan Island. In 1626 the Dutch paid Native Americans about $24 in goods for the island. Today it is New York City.

Section Wrap-Up

Answer these questions to check your understanding of the entire section.

1. **Determining Cause and Effect** What started the Protestant Reformation, and what was the result?

_____

_____

2. **Analyzing** Why did European nations compete for colonies in the Americas?

_____

_____

In the space below, write a brief narrative about one of the explorers who came in search of the Northwest Passage. Explain when and where the exploration took place, as well as the results of the exploration.

_____

_____

_____

_____

_____

_____

_____

_____

_____

_____

_____

_____

_____

_____

Early English Settlements

Essential Question

Why did the English settle in North America?

Directions: As you read, complete a graphic organizer like the one below to explain why the English settled in North America.

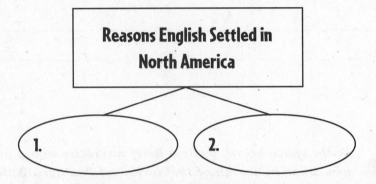

 **Notes**   **Read to Learn**

England in America *(pages 59–60)*

Sequencing

When did the English start setting up colonies in North America?

_____

_____

_____

_____

England and Spain had conflicts for many years before finally going to war. They had conflicts over trade and religious differences. King Philip II of Spain wanted a Catholic ruler in England. He did not think that Queen Elizabeth, a Protestant, was the rightful ruler. On the seas, Englishmen such as Francis Drake had attacked Spanish ships. Philip wanted Elizabeth to punish Drake. Instead, she made Drake a knight. In response, Philip sent the Spanish Armada, Spain's warships, to conquer England. The Spanish failed, and Spain lost control of the seas. Now England could start colonies in North America.

In 1584 Queen Elizabeth gave Sir Walter Raleigh the right to claim land in North America. He decided that Roanoke Island, off the coast of present-day North Carolina, was a good place to start a settlement. After a difficult first winter there, however, the 100 men who settled Roanoke returned to England. In 1587 Raleigh sent 91 men, 17 women, and 9 children to Roanoke. John White, a mapmaker, was their leader.

White returned to England to get more supplies. He planned on returning within a few months. However, the war between England and Spain delayed him. He did not return for nearly three years. When he returned, he found Roanoke Island deserted, and the colonists were never seen again.

Jamestown Settlement (pages 60–61)

Formulating Questions

As you read, ask yourself questions to make sure that you understand the text. Good questions begin with the words who, what, when, where, why, and how. Use one of these question words to write one question and answer about this passage in the space below.

_____

_____

_____

_____

_____

Identifying

What helped Jamestown make a profit?

_____

_____

_____

After Roanoke failed, the English did not plan new colonies for many years. But interest grew again in 1608. Some groups of merchants bought **charters,** documents granting the right to start settlements in an area, from King James I.

One group, the Virginia Company of London, was a **joint-stock company.** Investors bought stock in the company in return for a share of its future profits. The company wanted settlers in America to look for gold and establish trade.

Three ships from the Virginia Company entered Chesapeake Bay in April 1607 and sailed up a river. The colonists named the river James in honor of the king. They named the new settlement Jamestown.

Captain John Smith led the colony. He forced the settlers to work. He explored the area and got corn from the Native Americans. Powhatan was the Native American chief. When John Smith returned to England, Jamestown lost a strong leader. The colonists struggled to survive the harsh winter of 1609–1610.

Eventually the Jamestown settlers found a way to make money for the investors. They began to grow tobacco, and the colony earned a profit. The Virginia Company wanted people to leave England and settle in the colony. Settlers who paid their own way to Jamestown were given a **headright,** or land grant, of 50 acres.

The colony of Virginia grew and began to do well. Colonists participated in the colony's government. The House of Burgesses first met in 1619. The **burgesses** were representatives of the 10 towns who made local laws.

Women and children added to the growth of the colony. Slavery became an important part of the colony's economy when a Virginia law recognized it in the 1660s.

However by the 1620s, Jamestown was no longer making a profit. King James canceled the Virginia Company's charter. In 1624 Jamestown became England's first royal colony in America.

Section Wrap-Up

Answer these questions to check your understanding of the entire section.

1. **Determining Cause and Effect** What were two causes of conflict between England and Spain in the 1500s?

   _____

   _____

2. **Explaining** What actions did John Smith take to lead the Jamestown colony?

   _____

   _____

Persuasive Writing

In the space provided, write a letter to a friend in England as if you were a Jamestown settler. The letter should persuade your friend to come to Jamestown.

_____

_____

_____

_____

_____

_____

_____

_____

_____

_____

_____

_____

_____

_____

New England Colonies

Essential Question

Why did the Separatists and Puritans leave England and settle in North America?

Directions: As you read, complete a graphic organizer like the one below to explain why the Separatists and Puritans left England and settled in North America.

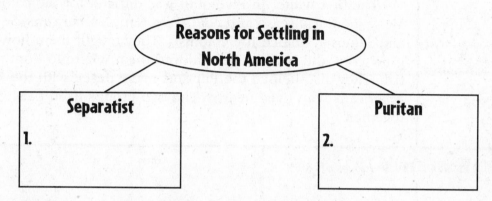

Reasons for Settling in North America

Separatist
1.

Puritan
2.

 **Notes**   # Read to Learn

Religious Freedom (pages 65–66)

Identifying Central Issues

What was a primary reason that colonists came to the Americas?

_____

_____

_____

The next group of colonists to come to America wanted religious freedom. England became a Protestant country in 1534, when King Henry VIII formed the Anglican Church. Some people were not happy with the new church. Many people **dissented,** or disagreed, with the beliefs or practices of the new church. Some Protestants wanted to change the Anglican Church. They were called **Puritans.** Others wanted to set up different churches. They were called **Separatists.**

The Separatists were persecuted in England, so they moved to the Netherlands. There they had religious freedom, but they could not find work. Some Separatists made an arrangement with the Virginia Company. They would settle in Virginia and practice their religion freely. In exchange, they would give the company a part of their profits.

The Separatists thought of themselves as **Pilgrims** because their journey had a religious purpose. They started their journey aboard the *Mayflower* in September 1620. Although they wanted to settle in the Virginia colony, they landed north of that colony. With winter approaching, the Pilgrims went ashore and settled

Religious Freedom (continued)

Speculating

What might have happened to the Pilgrims if Native Americans had not helped them?

_____

_____

_____

_____

in a place called Plymouth. Before leaving the ship, the Pilgrims drew up a document called the **Mayflower Compact.** In the document, the Pilgrims pledged to be loyal to England. They said that they planned to form a government, and they promised to obey the laws they passed. The Mayflower Compact was an important step in setting up representative government in the new American colonies.

The first winter in Plymouth was difficult for the colonists. Many died of disease and cold. Two Native Americans, Squanto and Samoset, helped the colonists. They taught them how to grow corn and beans. They showed them where to hunt and fish. They also helped the Pilgrims make peace with the Native Americans who lived nearby. The two groups lived peacefully together.

New Settlements (pages 67–69)

Identifying

What was the Great Migration?

_____

_____

_____

Charles I, who became king of England in 1625, disagreed with the Puritans call for changes in the Anglican Church. Puritans were persecuted, and some wanted to leave England. A group of Puritans formed the Massachusetts Bay Company in 1629. They received a charter to set up a colony north of Plymouth. In 1630 about 900 Puritans arrived in Massachusetts Bay and settled in a place they called Boston. John Winthrop was the colony's governor.

Thousands of Puritans came to Massachusetts in the 1630s. This movement became known as the Great Migration. One reason Puritans came to America was for religious freedom. They did not, however, tolerate religious beliefs that were different from their own. They persecuted people whose beliefs were different from theirs. Some persecuted people moved to the surrounding areas to form new colonies.

In 1636 Thomas Hooker, a Massachusetts minister, led his congregation to Connecticut. There he founded the town of Hartford. In 1639 Hartford and the towns of Windsor and Wethersfield formed a colony. They set up a plan of government called the **Fundamental Orders of Connecticut.** This was the first constitution in America. It set up a representative government.

Roger Williams, a minister, and other colonists who were forced out of Massachusetts formed the colony of Rhode Island. It was the first place in America where people of all faiths could worship freely.

New Settlements (continued)

 **Summarizing**

What colonies did Thomas Hooker and Roger Williams found?

Thomas Hooker:

_____

Roger Williams:

_____

Native Americans traded furs for the settlers' goods. However, conflict over land arose between the two groups. Usually settlers moved into Native American land without permission. War broke out in 1636. The Native Americans were defeated, and their power in New England was destroyed. The colonists began expanding their settlements.

Section Wrap-Up ***Answer these questions to check your understanding of the entire section.***

1. **Evaluating** Why was the Mayflower Compact an important document?

   _____

   _____

2. **Determining Cause and Effect** What was the result of the 1636 war between Native Americans and the New England colonists?

   _____

   _____

Expository Writing ***On a separate sheet of paper, write an essay that explains how the New England colonies were started.***

Middle Colonies

Essential Question

How did the Middle Colonies develop?

Directions: As you read, complete a graphic organizer like the one below to show how the Middle Colonies developed.

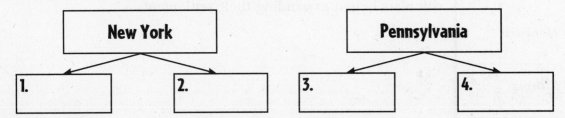

New York	Pennsylvania
1. ___ 2. ___	3. ___ 4. ___

Notes | Read to Learn

England and the Colonies (pages 73–74)

Identifying

Who first controlled New Netherland?

_____

_____

In 1660 England had two sets of colonies in what is now the United States. Massachusetts, New Hampshire, Connecticut, and Rhode Island were in the north. Maryland and Virginia were in the south. Between the two sets of colonies were lands controlled by the Dutch. They called the land New Netherland. The main settlement in New Netherland was called New Amsterdam. It was located on Manhattan Island. New Amsterdam had a good seaport and was the center for shipping.

The Dutch West India Company wanted more settlers to come to their colony. It offered large areas of land to anyone who could bring at least 50 settlers to work the land. The people who obtained the land were called **patroons.** They ruled like kings.

New Netherland had a good harbor. River trade made money for the Dutch. The English wanted New Netherland. They sent a fleet to attack it. Peter Stuyvesant, the colony's governor, surrendered without a fight.

King Charles II gave the colony to his brother, the Duke of York. He renamed it New York. New York was a **proprietary colony.** The proprietor, or owner, of the colony owned all the land and controlled the government. This differed from the New England colonies. There voters elected the governor and an assembly.

**Notes** | # Read to Learn

England and the Colonies *(continued)*

Comparing

What is the main difference between a proprietary colony and a royal colony?

_____

_____

_____

_____

In 1664 about 8,000 people lived in New York. By 1683, more than 12,000 people lived in the colony. New York City was one of the fastest-growing places in the colony.

The Duke of York gave the southern part of New York to two proprietors, who named their colony New Jersey. People from different ethnic backgrounds and religions lived in New York and New Jersey.

New Jersey did not have a port or large city like New York. Also, New Jersey's proprietors made few profits. By 1702, the proprietors had sold their shares in the colony. New Jersey became a royal colony. The king controlled the colony, but the colonists made local laws.

Pennsylvania *(page 75)*

Explaining

Why did William Penn receive land for a new colony in America?

_____

_____

_____

_____

William Penn was a wealthy English Quaker. In 1681 he received land in America from the king of England as payment for a debt that the king owed Penn's father. The new colony was named Pennsylvania. Penn saw Pennsylvania as a place where he could put his Quaker beliefs into practice. The Quakers believed that everyone was equal. They were also **pacifists,** or people who refuse to use force or to fight in wars. They were persecuted in England for their beliefs.

Penn designed the city of Philadelphia. He supervised the building of the city. He believed the land belonged to the Native Americans and the settlers should pay them for it. Settlers arrived from several European countries. The colony was governed by a Charter of Liberties. It gave colonists the right to elect representatives to the legislature.

Swedes had settled southern Pennsylvania before Penn formed the Pennsylvania colony. They were allowed to form their own legislatures. They operated as a separate colony known as Delaware under Pennsylvania's governor.

Section Wrap-Up

Answer these questions to check your understanding of the entire section.

1. **Comparing and Contrasting** How were the colonies of New York and New Jersey alike and different?

_____

_____

_____

2. **Drawing Conclusions** How did the colony of Pennsylvania reflect Quaker beliefs?

_____

_____

_____

Informative Writing

Imagine that you are a traveler in the Middle Colonies. Write an article that gives information about the colonies and how they were started.

_____

_____

_____

_____

_____

_____

_____

_____

_____

_____

_____

_____

_____

Chapter 3, Section 4 (Pages 76–82)
Southern Colonies

Essential Question

How and why did the Southern Colonies grow?

Directions: As you read, complete a chart like the one below to explain why the Southern Colonies were started.

Colony	Why Started?
Maryland	1.
Carolinas	2.
Georgia	3.

Notes | Read to Learn

Maryland and Virginia (pages 77–78)

Finding the Main Idea

Underline the main idea in each paragraph.

Plantations were important to the economy of the Southern Colonies. As the number of plantations grew, so did the need for workers. English criminals were shipped to the colonies. They earned their release by working for a length of time. African rulers sold their prisoners of war to European slave traders. They then took the enslaved people to the colonies. Many people also came to the colonies as **indentured servants.** They paid for their trip to the colonies by working without pay for a certain amount of time.

Maryland was a proprietary colony. The owner gave large pieces of land, called **estates,** to English aristocrats. Estate owners formed plantations. They brought indentured servants and enslaved Africans to work the land.

Maryland began as a safe place for Catholics, who were persecuted in England. However, Protestants were also welcome in Maryland. They soon outnumbered Catholics. To protect Catholics, Maryland passed the Act of Toleration. It gave Catholics and Protestants the right to worship freely. But in 1692, Maryland's assembly made the Anglican Church the official church of Maryland. Catholics then faced the same problems they had in England.

During this time, the Virginia colony continued to grow. Settlers moved West and took over Native American lands. To stop conflicts, Virginia's governor made a deal with Native

Chapter 3, Section 4

31

Copyright © Glencoe/McGraw-Hill, a division of The McGraw-Hill Companies, Inc.

Maryland and Virginia (continued)

Americans. He promised to keep settlers from moving west. But many Virginians ignored this deal. Some settled in the forbidden lands. In 1676 Nathaniel Bacon, a Virginia planter, led attacks on Native Americans. Bacon's Rebellion, as the attacks were called, showed that settlers would not be stopped from moving onto Native American lands.

The Carolinas and Georgia (pages 79–80)

Contrasting

How were North Carolina and South Carolina different?

_____

_____

_____

_____

In 1663 King Charles II created the proprietary colony of Carolina. The proprietors sold land to English settlers. John Locke, an English philosopher, wrote the colony's **constitution,** or plan of government. But Carolina did not develop as planned. It split into North Carolina and South Carolina. Farmers from Virginia settled North Carolina. There they grew tobacco and sold timber and tar. North Carolina lacked good harbors. It used Virginia harbors for trade. South Carolina had fertile farmland and good harbors. Rice and indigo, a plant used to dye textiles, were important crops in the Carolinas.

Georgia was founded in 1733 as a colony for debtors and those with little money who wanted to make a fresh start. **Debtors** are people who were not able to repay debts. The British also hoped that Georgia, which was located north of Spanish Florida, would protect the other colonies from Spain.

The French and Spanish in North America (pages 81–82)

Identifying

Name the French explorers who explored the Mississippi River.

1. _____

2. _____

3. _____

In addition to Britain, France and Spain also set up settlements in North America. The French founded Quebec in 1608. The French were not interested in large settlements. They were mainly interested in fishing and fur trading. In 1663 New France became a royal colony. Louis Joliet and Jacques Marquette explored part of the Mississippi River. René-Robert Cavelier, Sieur de La Salle, explored the Mississippi River all the way to the Gulf of Mexico. He claimed the region for France and called it Louisiana, in honor of King Louis XIV.

New France was made up of estates along the St. Lawrence River. Estate owners employed **tenant farmers.** Tenant farmers paid the estate owner an annual rent and worked for him for a certain number of days each year. The French got along better with Native Americans than other Europeans. The French lived among the Native Americans, learned their language, and respected their ways.

The French and Spanish in North America *(continued)*

 **Analyzing**

How did the Spanish treat Native Americans in their missions in North America?

_____

_____

_____

_____

In the early 1600s, the Spanish controlled most of Mexico, the Caribbean, and Central and South America. The Spanish also sent soldiers, missionaries, and settlers north into present-day New Mexico. They moved into what is now Texas. Spanish priests built missions along the Pacific coast. **Missions** are religious settlements that were set up to convert people to a faith. In addition to converting Native Americans to Christianity, the Spanish also forced them to work in the fields and workshops.

The missions helped the Spanish to claim California. Many missions later became cities, such as Los Angeles and Monterrey.

Section Wrap-Up *Answer these questions to check your understanding of the entire section.*

1. **Listing** Name three types of workers who were employed on plantations.

   _____

   _____

2. **Contrasting** How did the French settlement of North America differ from that of other European countries?

   _____

   _____

Descriptive Writing *On a separate sheet of paper, write a journal entry as if you were a settler in one of the Southern Colonies. Describe the colony, and explain why you settled there.*

Chapter 4, Section 1 (Pages 88–95)
Life in the Colonies

Essential Question

How did geography affect the economic development of the three colonial regions?

Directions: As you read, complete a graphic organizer like the one below to explain how geography affected the economy of the colonies.

Colonies	Geography	Economic Activities
New England	1.	2.
Middle	3.	4.
Southern	5.	6.

 **Notes** | **Read to Learn**

The New England Colonies (pages 89–91)

Listing

What were the three main economic activities in New England?

1._____

2._____

3._____

The number of people in the American colonies grew between 1607 and 1775. About 1 million Europeans and Africans came to the colonies during this time. Another reason for this increase was that colonial women married early and had big families. New England, and other places in America, were healthy places to live.

The main economic activity in New England was farming. New England, however, had poor soil and long winters. The farms were small, and farmers practiced **subsistence farming.** They produced just enough to meet the needs of their families.

Shipbuilding was an important industry. Ships were built with the lumber from nearby forests. Fishing was also an important part of the New England economy. The coastal cities were the center of the shipping trade. They linked America to other parts of the world.

Some colonial merchants followed shipping routes that became known as the **triangular trade.** These routes formed a triangle. On one part of the journey, ships brought sugar and molasses from the West Indies to New England. In New England, the molasses was made into rum. The rum and other goods were shipped to West Africa and traded for enslaved Africans. The cruel part of the triangular trade was the **Middle Passage,** when enslaved Africans were shipped to the West.

Notes | Read to Learn

The Middle Colonies (page 92)

Stating

Why did the Middle Colonies have so many cultures?

_____

_____

_____

_____

The soil in the Middle Colonies was more fertile and the climate was milder than in New England. Farmers in the Middle Colonies grew **cash crops.** These crops were used by the farmers' families, but they were also sold in the colonies and overseas. Cash crops were shipped from cities such as New York City and Philadelphia, which became busy ports.

The Middle Colonies also had industries such as lumbering and manufacturing. About 100,000 Germans came to the American colonies. Most of them settled in Pennsylvania, where they became successful farmers. Many non-English people also came to the Middle Colonies.

The Southern Colonies and Slavery (pages 93–95)

Comparing and Contrasting

How were the Tidewater and the backcountry alike and different?

_____

_____

_____

_____

_____

The Southern Colonies had rich soil and a warm climate, which made these colonies well suited for farming. The Southern Colonies had little industry. Tobacco was the main cash crop of Maryland and Virginia. At first, tobacco planters used indentured servants to work in the fields. Later the planters began using enslaved Africans for labor. Slaveholders became rich from growing tobacco. Sometimes there was a **surplus,** or extra amount, of tobacco on the market. This caused tobacco prices to fall and the planters' profits to fall as well. The main cash crop in South Carolina and Georgia was rice. Rice was grown in low-lying areas, in fields called paddies. Growing rice was hard work. The rice growers relied on enslaved Africans for labor.

Most of the large Southern plantations were located in the **Tidewater.** This was a region of low-lying plains along the seacoast. Each plantation was like a little town. It had fields stretching around a group of buildings, such as barns, stables, slave cabins, and carpenter shops.

West of the Tidewater was the **backcountry.** This was a region of hills and forests near the Appalachian Mountains. Settlers in the backcountry grew corn and tobacco on small farms. Farmers here usually worked with their families. There were more backcountry farmers than large plantation owners. However, the plantation owners were wealthier. They controlled the economy of the region.

Most enslaved Africans lived on plantations, where they were treated cruelly. Most worked in the fields. The large plantation owners hired **overseers.** These were bosses who kept the enslaved Africans working hard.

The Southern Colonies and Slavery (continued)

Finding the Main Idea

To identify the main idea of each paragraph, underline key words or phrases.

Many of the colonies set up **slave codes.** These codes were rules that controlled enslaved Africans. They usually called for enslaved people to be whipped or killed for offenses. Most white Southerners were not slaveholders, but slavery was important to the Southern economy. There was less support for slavery in the Northern Colonies. Eventually, the conflict over slavery would lead to a war between the North and South.

Section Wrap-Up

Answer these questions to check your understanding of the entire section.

1. **Determining Cause and Effect** What were three reasons for population growth in the New England colonies?

   _____

   _____

2. **Drawing Conclusions** Why did slavery become an important part of the economy of the Southern Colonies?

   _____

   _____

Persuasive Writing

Choose one of the three colonial regions. As a colonist in that region, write a letter to a friend in England. Persuade the friend to come to the region in which you live. Include reasons why the region is a desirable place to live. Explain why it is a more desirable place to live than the other two colonial regions. Write your letter on a separate sheet of paper.

Government, Religion, Culture

Essential Question

In what ways was an American culture developing during the colonial period?

Directions: As you read, complete a graphic organizer like the one below to explain how the Great Awakening, education, and the Enlightenment affected the colonists.

| Great Awakening ⟹ | 1. | Education ⟹ | 2. | Enlightenment ⟹ | 3. |

Notes | Read to Learn

English Colonial Rule (pages 99–100)

Explaining

What were the Navigation Acts?

_____

_____

_____

James II was the English king in the mid-1600s. He tried to take back the powers that Parliament had won during the English Civil War. He also tried to tighten control over the American colonies. Parliament decided to replace him with his daughter Mary and her husband William. In 1689, William and Mary signed an English Bill of Rights that guaranteed basic rights to all citizens.

England wanted to make money from trade. To do so, it wanted to **export,** or sell, more goods to foreign countries than it **imported,** or bought from them. England used the raw materials from the colonies, such as lumber, to manufacture goods. England then sold the manufactured goods to the colonists.

England passed the Navigation Acts to direct trade between England and the colonies. Under these laws, the colonists could not use foreign ships to send goods to England even if those ships had cheaper shipping rates. The Navigation Acts would not allow colonists to sell certain products, such as sugar or tobacco, to any country other than England.

At first the colonists didn't mind the laws. The laws provided for a place to sell their raw materials. Later they began to resent these laws. They wanted to make their own goods and sell them where they could get the highest prices.

Notes | Read to Learn

Colonial Government (pages 100–101)

Identifying

Who elected the governor and legislature in charter colonies?

_____

_____

By the 1600s, English people had won several rights, such as the right to a trial by jury. The English also believed in limited government and in representative government. The idea of a limited government was established in the Magna Carta in 1215. The Magna Carta also protected against unjust punishment and against the loss of life, liberty, and property.

By the 1760s, there were three kinds of colonies in America. Each kind had its own small government. Connecticut and Rhode Island were **charter colonies.** Settlers were given a charter to set up these colonies. Colonists there elected their own governors and members of the legislature, or lawmaking body.

Delaware, Maryland, and Pennsylvania were **proprietary colonies.** They were ruled by proprietors, individuals or groups who received land grants from Britain. Proprietors appointed the governor and some members of the legislature.

Georgia, Massachusetts, New Hampshire, New Jersey, New York, North Carolina, South Carolina, and Virginia were **royal colonies.** The king directly ruled these colonies. In each, he appointed a governor and part of the legislature.

Legislatures generally gave the right to vote only to white men who owned property. Even so, the number of people involved in government was greater in the colonies than in Europe.

An Emerging Culture (pages 102–103)

Comparing and Contrasting

Complete the following sentences about men's and women's roles in the colonies:

Men

_____

_____

Women

_____

_____

The Great Awakening was a religious revival in the colonies in the 1700s. Ministers called for a return to a strong faith. The Great Awakening led to the start of many new churches.

The family was the foundation of colonial society. Men were the formal heads of the households. They worked in the fields and built barns and houses. Women ran the households and raised the children. Married women were under their husband's authority and had few rights. Widows and unmarried women could run businesses and own property, but women could not vote.

Education was important to the colonists. Parents often taught their children to read and write at home. In the 1600s, Puritans in Massachusetts passed a law requiring that larger towns have schools. By 1750, most men and women in New England could read. Widows, unmarried women, Quakers, and other religious groups ran many schools. The first colleges in the colonies were started to train ministers.

An Emerging Culture (continued)

Describing

What was the Enlightenment?

_____

_____

_____

By the mid-1700s, Enlightenment ideas became important to many colonists. They thought that knowledge, reason, and science could improve society. This movement increased interest in science in the colonies. People observed nature, set up experiments, and reported their findings. The best-known American scientist was Benjamin Franklin.

In 1735 John Peter Zenger of the *New York Weekly Journal* went to court to face charges of libel. The charges were based on comments he wrote about the royal governor of New York. Andrew Hamilton defended Zenger. Hamilton argued that free speech was a basic right of English people. A jury found Zenger not guilty. This was an important step in the development of a free press.

Section Wrap-Up

Answer these questions to check your understanding of the entire section.

1. **Analyzing** How did the colonists' view of the Navigation Acts change?

_____

_____

2. **Contrasting** How were the governments in charter, proprietary, and royal colonies different?

_____

_____

Expository Writing

On a separate sheet of paper, write a brief essay that explains how English principles influenced colonial government.

France and Britain Clash

Essential Question

Why did conflict arise in North America between France and Great Britain?

Directions: As you read, complete a graphic organizer like the one below to explain the causes of conflict in North America between France and Great Britain.

Causes

1. ☐
2. ☐
3. ☐

→

Effect

French-British Conflict

 **Notes** | **Read to Learn**

British-French Rivalry (pages 105–106)

Drawing Conclusions

Why did the Native Americans in the American colonies often help the French?

_____

_____

_____

During the 1700s, Britain and France were two of the strongest powers in Europe. They competed for wealth and land in different parts of the world. This caused bitterness between British and French colonists in North America. The French did not want to share their fur trade in the Ohio Valley with the British. The British built a fort at a place called Pickawillany. The French attacked the fort and drove the British out of Ohio.

Both the French and British wanted Native Americans as allies. The French traders had close ties with Native Americans through the fur trade. Unlike the British, the French did not want to take over Native American lands. As a result, Native Americans most often helped the French against the British.

The **Iroquois Confederacy** in the New York area was a powerful group of Native Americans. The confederacy traded with both the British and the French. It played one side against the other. By the mid-1700s, however, the confederacy gave trading rights to the British and reluctantly became British allies. This upset the balance of power between Britain and France.

 **Notes**

Read to Learn

American Colonists Take Action (pages 106–107)

Explaining

Why were George Washington and the militia ordered to build a fort near present-day Pittsburgh?

_____

_____

_____

_____

A group of Virginians wanted to settle the Ohio Valley. In 1753 the Governor of Virginia sent George Washington to take a message to the French. Washington was to tell them that they were trespassing on land the British claimed and they should leave. The French refused. Washington was sent back to the Ohio country with a **militia,** a group of civilian soldiers. The militia was ordered to build a fort on the site of present-day Pittsburgh. When Washington and the troops arrived, they found that the French were already building Fort Duquesne (doo•KAYN). Washington created his own post nearby, called Fort Necessity.

The French troops outnumbered Washington's militia. Washington attacked the French, but he was forced to surrender. Washington and his troops were later released and returned to Virginia. Washington published an account of these events. This made him famous throughout the colonies and Europe. He became a hero to the colonists because he had struck a blow against the French.

In 1754 representatives from several colonies met in Albany, New York. They talked about a way to defend themselves against the French. They hoped to get the Iroquois to support the British. The representatives approved Benjamin Franklin's Albany Plan of Union. This plan called for a united colonial government. Every colonial legislature disapproved of the plan. The colonies did not want to give up any of their power. The colonists did not unite against the French. Soon a full-scale war began called the French and Indian War.

Section Wrap-Up

Answer these questions to check your understanding of the entire section.

1. **Making Inferences** Why do you think the Iroquois were slow to become allies with the British?

   _____

   _____

2. **Identifying Points of View** Why did colonial legislatures oppose the Albany Plan of Union?

   _____

   _____

In the space provided, write an article for a British newspaper. As a British colonist, explain the reasons for the growing conflict between the British and the French in the colonies.

_____

_____

_____

_____

_____

_____

_____

_____

_____

_____

_____

_____

_____

The French and Indian War

Essential Question

How did the outcome of the French and Indian War determine who controlled North America?

Directions: As you read, complete a graphic organizer like the one below to list the lands France lost as a result of the Treaty of Paris of 1763.

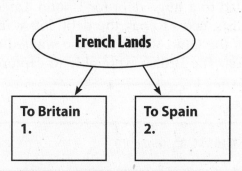

French Lands

To Britain
1.

To Spain
2.

Notes

Read to Learn

The British Take Action (pages 109–111)

Formulating Questions

As you read, ask yourself questions to make sure that you understand the text. Begin with the words who, what, when, where, why, *and* how. *Use one of the question words to write one question and answer about this passage.*

_____

_____

_____

_____

_____

The British and the French were in a struggle to control world trade and sea power. The French and Indian War was part of this larger conflict. The French were building forts throughout the Ohio River valley and the Great Lakes region. The French **alliances,** or unions, with Native Americans helped them control large areas of land. These areas stretched from the St. Lawrence River in Canada to New Orleans.

At first the British colonists fought the French and the Native Americans with little help from Britain. Then in 1754, the British government joined the fight. The government appointed General Edward Braddock to be in charge of British forces in America. He was to drive the French out of the Ohio River valley.

In 1755 Braddock set out to attack the French at Fort Duquesne. He had a force of British soldiers and some militia. George Washington went along. Washington told Braddock that the British style of marching was a problem. The British soldiers made good targets. They lined up in columns and rows in bright red uniforms. This was not a good way to fight on the frontier. Braddock ignored this advice. The French attacked and defeated the British. General Braddock was killed.

The fighting in the colonies started a new war in Europe called the Seven Years' War. The British and French fought each

 **Notes** | **Read to Learn**

The British Take Action (continued)

other in different parts of the world. French forces captured several British forts in America. They drove many British settlers back to the coast.

When William Pitt became the prime minister of Great Britain, the British were more successful. Pitt was a good military planner. He decided to pay for all the necessary war supplies. This led to a huge debt for Britain. Later Britain would raise the colonists' taxes to pay the debt. Pitt wanted to drive the French out of the Ohio Valley. He also wanted to conquer French Canada. The British were able to capture several French forts.

The Fall of New France (page 111)

In 1759 British troops marched on Quebec, the capital of New France. In 1760 the British captured Montreal. This brought an end to fighting in North America. The Treaty of Paris of 1763 forced France to give Canada and most lands east of the Mississippi River to Great Britain. Spain received French lands west of the Mississippi River. The treaty marked the end of France as a power in North America.

Trouble on the Frontier (page 112)

Determining Causes

Why did the British government issue the Proclamation of 1763?

_____

_____

_____

_____

The French loss hurt Native Americans. More British settlers began moving onto Native American lands. Pontiac was a Native American leader. He tried to unite Native Americans to fight the British. In 1763 he captured several British forts. There was fighting all along the Pennsylvania and Virginia frontiers. In 1765 the British defeated Pontiac's allies. This ended Pontiac's War. Pontiac signed a treaty with the British.

Britain wanted to avoid more conflicts with Native Americans. Britain issued the Proclamation of 1763. It said settlers could not move west of the Appalachian Mountains. The proclamation angered colonists. It especially angered **speculators,** or investors. These people had already bought western lands. More conflicts would soon develop between Britain and the colonists.

Section Wrap-Up

Answer these questions to check your understanding of the entire section.

1. **Speculating** Why do you think General Braddock ignored General Washington's advice about how the British troops should march on the colonial frontier?

   _____

   _____

2. **Synthesizing** How did the actions of William Pitt contribute to later conflicts between the British and the American colonists?

   _____

   _____

Persuasive Writing

Take on the role of Pontiac. In the space provided, write a speech calling on Native Americans to unite to fight the British. Give reasons why Native Americans should fight.

_____

_____

_____

_____

_____

_____

_____

_____

_____

_____

_____

_____

_____

_____

_____

_____

Taxation Without Representation

Essential Question

Following the French and Indian War, how did the British government anger the American colonists?

Directions: As you read, complete a graphic organizer like the one below to identify British policies that affected the colonists and the colonists' view of these policies.

British Policy   **Colonists' View**

1.	⟶	2.
3.	⟶	4.
5.	⟶	6.

Notes   Read to Learn

Relations With Britain (pages 123–124)

Explaining

Why did the British place new taxes on the colonists?

_____

_____

_____

_____

_____

After the French and Indian War, the British gained a huge area in North America. To help control this territory, the British government issued the Proclamation of 1763. This proclamation set up new provinces in Canada, Florida, and the Caribbean. It also said that colonists could not move west of the Appalachian Mountains. This helped avoid conflict with Native Americans, and it allowed Britain to control the fur trade. By keeping the colonists near the Atlantic coast, the proclamation helped British trade with the colonies to grow.

Britain placed 10,000 troops in the colonies to protect its interests there. It needed **revenue,** or incoming money, to pay the troops. Britain also had a huge debt from the French and Indian War. The British believed the colonists should help pay some of the cost. As a result, the British government placed new taxes on the colonists. It also began to make sure that all taxes were paid.

Some colonists smuggled goods to avoid paying taxes. In 1763 the British prime minister, George Grenville, decided to stop the smuggling. He knew that American juries often found smugglers innocent. Grenville convinced Parliament to pass a law that sent smugglers to courts that were run by officers and did not

Relations With Britain (continued)

Drawing Conclusions

What right of British citizens did the writs of assistance violate?

_____

_____

have juries. Parliament also approved **writs of assistance.** These documents allowed officers to search any location for smuggled goods.

In 1764 Parliament passed the Sugar Act. This law lowered the tax on imported molasses. The British hoped the colonists would pay this lower tax instead of smuggling. The law also allowed officers to take goods from smugglers without going to court. The colonists believed that the Sugar Act and the other new laws violated their rights as British citizens. These rights included the right to a jury trial and the right to be safe in their own homes. Many colonists also believed that they should not be taxed if they did not agree to the taxes.

New Taxes (pages 124–125)

Determining Cause and Effect

Complete the sentences below to explain the chain of events that led Parliament to repeal the Stamp Act.

Colonial merchants
_____
_____
_____

↓

British merchants
_____
_____
_____

↓

Parliament repealed the Stamp Act.

In 1765 Parliament passed the Stamp Act, which placed a tax on printed materials, such as newspapers. The colonists did not agree with this act. It interfered in colonial affairs, and the colonists had not agreed to the tax. In Virginia, Patrick Henry convinced the House of Burgesses to pass a **resolution,** or a formal expression of opinion. The resolution said that only the Virginia assembly had the power to tax the citizens of Virginia. In Boston, Samuel Adams helped start the Sons of Liberty. This group protested the Stamp Act. Protesters burned **effigies,** or rag figures, that represented tax collectors.

In October delegates, or representatives, from nine colonies met in New York. This meeting was called the Stamp Act Congress. The delegates sent a petition to Parliament and the British king. It said that only the colonies' own assemblies could tax the colonists. Colonial merchants decided to **boycott,** or refuse to buy, British goods. Many merchants signed **nonimportation** agreements. These were pledges not to buy or use goods imported from Britain. British merchants began to lose business. They asked Parliament to **repeal,** or cancel, the Stamp Act. Parliament repealed that law but passed another law saying that Parliament had the right to tax the colonists.

In 1767 Parliament passed the Townshend Acts. These laws placed taxes on goods that were imported to the colonies. By this time, any taxes passed by Britain angered the colonists. Groups like the Daughters of Liberty encouraged Americans to produce their own goods instead of buying British goods.

Section Wrap-Up

Answer these questions to check your understanding of the entire section.

1. **Explaining** Why did the colonists oppose the Stamp Act and other taxes?

_____

_____

_____

2. **Defending** Do you think the British Parliament was justified, or right, in taxing the colonists? Why or why not?

_____

_____

_____

Persuasive Writing

In the space provided, write a newspaper editorial urging colonists to produce their own goods instead of buying British goods. Provide reasons why you believe this is in the best interest of the colonies.

_____

_____

_____

_____

_____

_____

_____

_____

_____

_____

_____

_____

Building Colonial Unity

Essential Question

How did colonists react to British policies?

Directions: As you read, complete a graphic organizer like the one below to show how the colonists reacted to each of the British policies listed.

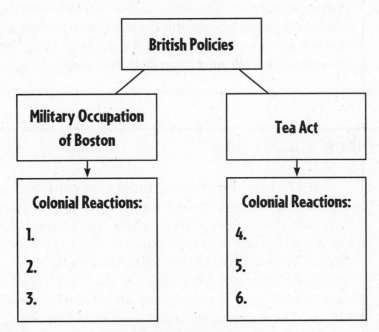

British Policies

Military Occupation of Boston → Colonial Reactions:
1.
2.
3.

Tea Act → Colonial Reactions:
4.
5.
6.

 Notes · Read to Learn

Trouble in Boston (pages 127–128)

Explaining

Why did the people of Boston resent the British soldiers?

_____

_____

_____

_____

_____

The colonists' protests started to make British officials nervous. Parliament decided to send troops to Boston to keep order. The colonists believed that the British had gone too far. To make matters worse, the British soldiers sometimes stole items and treated the colonists rudely.

On March 5, 1770, a fight broke out between the soldiers and Bostonians. Some Bostonians went to the customhouse, where British taxes were collected. They threw sticks and stones at the soldiers on duty. The soldiers became nervous and fired their guns into the crowd. Five colonists were killed. One of them was Crispus Attucks, a dockworker who was part African and part Native American. The colonists called this event the Boston Massacre.

Trouble in Boston (continued)

Identifying

Identify one example of propaganda described in this section.

_____

_____

The colonists used the killings as **propaganda,** or information used to influence public opinion. Samuel Adams put up posters showing the soldiers killing the Bostonians. Many colonists called for stronger boycotts. Parliament responded by repealing most of the Townshend Acts, but it kept the tax on tea.

In 1772 Samuel Adams brought back the Boston **committee of correspondence.** This organization spread writings about colonists' complaints against the British. The committees of correspondence soon spread throughout the colonies. They brought together the colonists who were against British policies.

A Crisis Over Tea (pages 128–129)

Formulating Questions

As you read this passage, ask yourself questions to make sure that you understand the text. Good questions begin with the words who, what, when, where, why, and how. *Use one of these question words to write one question and answer about this passage in the space below.*

Question:

_____

_____

Answer:

_____

_____

In 1773 the British East India Company was in trouble. Parliament wanted to save the company, so it passed the Tea Act. This law let the company ship tea to the colonies without paying the taxes normally paid on tea. It also let the company bypass colonial merchants and sell directly to shopkeepers. This made the company's tea cheaper than any other tea in the colonies. It also gave the company an advantage over colonial merchants. The merchants called for a new boycott.

The East India Company continued to ship tea to the colonies. The colonists forced some ships to turn back. Then three tea ships arrived in Boston Harbor. The royal governor ordered the ships to be unloaded. During the night of December 16, 1773, the Sons of Liberty dressed up as Mohawks. They boarded the ships and threw the tea overboard. This event became known as the Boston Tea Party.

King George III felt that Britain was losing control of the colonies. The British government passed the Coercive Acts to punish the colonists. These laws closed Boston Harbor until the colonists paid for the tea they threw overboard. This prevented food and other supplies from arriving at the harbor. The laws also banned most town meetings and forced Bostonians to keep British soldiers in their homes. Colonists believed that the Coercive Acts violated their rights as British citizens. They called them the Intolerable Acts.

Section Wrap-Up

Answer these questions to check your understanding of the entire section.

1. **Evaluating** How did the Boston Massacre help the colonists' cause?

_____

_____

_____

2. **Determining Cause and Effect** How did the British government respond to the Boston Tea Party?

_____

_____

_____

Descriptive Writing

In the space provided, write a letter that describes the situation in Boston after the British soldiers arrived. Write the letter as if you are a Bostonian writing to a relative back in England. Describe how the colonists are being treated and how they are reacting to the treatment.

_____

_____

_____

_____

_____

_____

_____

_____

_____

_____

_____

_____

_____

Chapter 5, Section 3 (Pages 132–137)

A Call to Arms

Essential Question

What brought about the clash between American colonists and British soldiers at Lexington and Concord?

Directions: As you read, complete a graphic organizer like the one below to list the events that led to the clash between American colonists and British soldiers at Lexington and Concord.

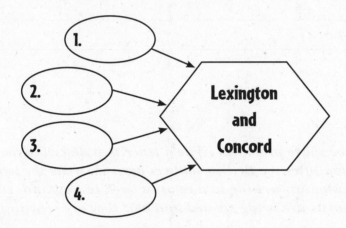

Notes	Read to Learn

The Continental Congress (page 133)

List three decisions of the Continental Congress in September 1774.

1. _____

   _____

2. _____

   _____

3. _____

   _____

Fifty-five delegates met in Philadelphia in September 1774. They came from all of the colonies except Georgia. They met to set up an organization that would challenge British control. The organization was called the Continental Congress. Leaders who attended the meeting included John Adams, Samuel Adams, Patrick Henry, John Jay, Richard Henry Lee, and George Washington. The delegates issued a statement that asked Parliament to repeal 13 acts that violated the colonists' rights. The delegates also voted to boycott trade with Britain. This included goods coming into and going out of the colonies.

The Continental Congress called on people to arm themselves against the British. The people formed **militias,** or groups of citizen soldiers. Militia companies in Massachusetts began to train and stockpile weapons. Some militia companies claimed that they would be ready to fight on a minute's notice. These companies became known as **minutemen.**

Read to Learn

The First Battles (pages 134–135)

Sequencing

Number the following events in the order in which they happened.

____ *Paul Revere and Richard Dawes warn Lexington that the British are coming.*

____ *King George declares that the colonies are in rebellion.*

____ *British troops are ordered to destroy the Massachusetts militia's weapons.*

The British also prepared for fighting. King George declared that the New England colonies were rebelling. By April 1775, several thousand British soldiers were stationed in and around Boston. The British general in charge had orders to get rid of the militia's weapons and arrest their leaders. He heard that the militia was storing weapons at Concord, a town near Boston. On April 18, 1775, he sent 700 troops to destroy the weapons and ammunition there.

People in Boston were watching the British soldiers. Two members of the Sons of Liberty, Paul Revere and William Dawes, rode to Lexington, a town near Concord. They warned the people there that the British were coming.

When the British neared Lexington, about 70 minutemen met them. Someone fired a shot, and then both sides began shooting. Eight minutemen were killed. The British moved on to Concord. When they arrived, they found that most of the militia's gunpowder had been removed. They destroyed the supplies that were left. Then the minutemen forced them to turn back.

Messengers had warned colonists from Boston to Concord about the British movements. As the British soldiers marched from Concord back to Boston, the militia fired on them. By the time the soldiers reached Boston, 73 were dead and at least 174 were wounded.

More Military Action (pages 136–137)

Making Connections

What does it mean when someone is called a "Benedict Arnold"? Why?

_____

_____

_____

After Lexington and Concord, many volunteers joined the militias. Benedict Arnold, a captain in the Connecticut militia, raised 400 men to capture Fort Ticonderoga on Lake Champlain. He joined Ethan Allen and the Vermont militia, known as the Green Mountain Boys. The two militias caught the British by surprise. Fort Ticonderoga surrendered on May 10, 1775. Later in the war, Arnold sold military information to the British. When this was discovered, he fled to New York City. There he commanded British troops and fought against the Americans.

The militia around Boston soon numbered about 20,000. On June 16, 1775, about 1,200 militiamen took up positions at Bunker Hill and Breed's Hill, across from Boston Harbor. The next day the British troops charged up Breed's Hill. The Americans fired at the soldiers, and they retreated. The British tried two more times and were fired on again. In the end, the Americans ran out of gunpowder and had to pull back. The British won the Battle of Bunker Hill, but more than 1,000 British soldiers died or were wounded.

More Military Action (continued)

Contrasting

Complete the follow-ing sentences:

Loyalists felt that

_____

_____

Patriots felt that

_____

_____

The colonists soon heard about these battles. They had to decide whether to join the rebels or stay loyal to Britain. Those who chose to stay with Britain were called **Loyalists.** They did not feel that unfair taxes and laws were enough reasons to rebel. Many of them expected that the British would win the war. **Patriots** were colonists who supported the war for independence. They felt that they could no longer live under British rule. The American Revolution was not just a war between the British and the Americans. It was also a war between the Patriots and Loyalists.

Section Wrap-Up

Answer these questions to check your understanding of the entire section.

1. **Determining Cause and Effect** What effect did the fighting at Lexington and Concord have on the militias?

   _____

   _____

2. **Analyzing** Explain why the American Revolution can be considered a civil war—a war between citizens of the same country.

   _____

   _____

   _____

Informative Writing

On a separate sheet of paper, write a newspaper article about the Battle of Bunker Hill. Tell what happened, when it happened, and who was involved.

Moving Toward Independence

Essential Question

Why did the American colonies choose to declare independence?

Directions: As you read, complete a graphic organizer like the one below to explain why the American colonies chose to declare independence.

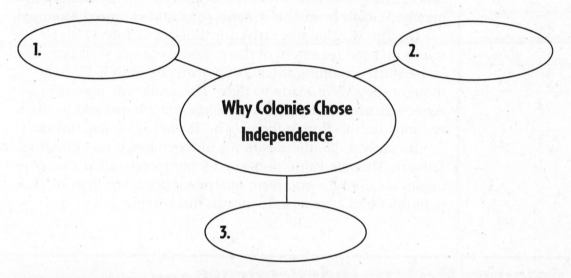

 **Notes** | **Read to Learn**

Colonial Leaders Emerge (pages 139–140)

Identifying

Name five of the delegates to the Second Continental Congress.

1. _____
2. _____
3. _____
4. _____
5. _____

The Second Continental Congress met on May 10, 1775. The delegates included some of the greatest political leaders in America. Some, like Patrick Henry and George Washington, were delegates to the First Continental Congress. Several new delegates also attended the Second Continental Congress. They included Benjamin Franklin, John Hancock, and Thomas Jefferson.

The Second Continental Congress began to govern the colonies. It decided to print money and set up a post office. It also set up committees to communicate with Native Americans and other countries. Most important, it created the Continental Army. This army would be able to fight the British in a more organized way than the militias could. The Congress chose George Washington to be the commander of the army.

Colonial Leaders Emerge (continued)

Evaluating

How successful was George Washington in training the Continental Army? Explain your answer.

_____

_____

_____

_____

The Congress offered Britain one more chance to avoid war. It sent a **petition,** or formal request, to King George III. This was called the Olive Branch Petition. It told the king that the colonists wanted peace and asked him to protect the colonists' rights. However, the king refused to receive the petition. Instead, he began to prepare for war.

In the meantime, the Congress learned that British troops in what is now Canada were planning to invade New York. The Americans decided to strike the British first. An American force marched north from Fort Ticonderoga and captured Montreal.

George Washington arrived in Boston in July 1775. He found that the members of the militia were not well organized, so he started training them as an army. By March 1776, he thought they were ready to fight. The army was placed in a semicircle around Boston. The soldiers were ordered to fire cannons on the British forces. The British army left Boston.

By early 1776, the desire for independence was growing. In January, Thomas Paine published a pamphlet called *Common Sense.* It called for complete independence from Britain. The pamphlet had a great influence in the colonies.

The Colonies Declare Independence (pages 141–142)

Summarizing

Briefly summarize the four parts of the Declaration of Independence.

1._____

_____

2._____

_____

3._____

_____

4._____

_____

At the meeting in Philadelphia, the Second Continental Congress debated whether or not the colonies should declare independence. The Congress decided to have a committee prepare a Declaration of Independence. The committee asked Thomas Jefferson to write the declaration.

On July 2, 1776, the Congress finally voted for independence. It approved the Declaration of Independence on July 4. The Declaration had four main parts. The **preamble,** or introduction, stated that people who want to form a new country should explain why. The second part listed the rights the colonists believed they should have. The third part listed the colonists' complaints against Britain. This part said that Britain had cut off the colonists' trade. It said that Parliament taxed the colonists without their approval. It also said that the colonists asked the king to address these problems, but he refused. The final part declared that the American colonies were a new nation.

Section Wrap-Up

Answer these questions to check your understanding of the entire section.

1. **Analyzing** How did the Second Continental Congress show that it was governing the colonies?

_____

_____

2. **Drawing Conclusions** Why did the colonists send King George III the Olive Branch Petition?

_____

_____

In the space provided, write a letter to convince a friend that independence from Britain is necessary. Write as if you are a colonist living in Boston and your friend is a colonist in another part of New England. Give your reasons for supporting independence.

_____

_____

_____

_____

_____

_____

_____

_____

_____

_____

_____

_____

_____

_____

Chapter 6, Section 1 (Pages 152–159)
The Early Years

Essential Question

What challenges did the American revolutionaries face at the start of the war?

Directions: As you read, complete a graphic organizer like the one below to list the challenges faced by the American revolutionaries at the start of the war.

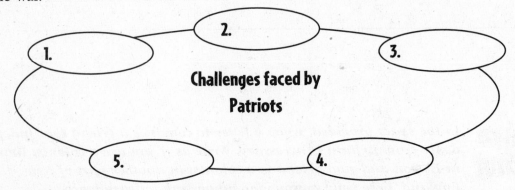

1.

2.

3.

Challenges faced by Patriots

5.

4.

Notes

Read to Learn

The Opposing Sides (pages 153–155)

Determining Cause and Effect

Why did the British think the war would be over quickly?

_____

_____

_____

Organizing

Circle the Patriot advantages. Underline the Patriot disadvantages.

War could not be avoided after the Declaration of Independence. The British had many advantages. They had the strongest navy in the world and a well-trained army. They also had a large and wealthy empire. The British thought their military would quickly put down the rebellion.

The Patriots had serious disadvantages. The colonies did not have a regular army or a strong navy. The army did not have enough weapons or ammunition, and not all Americans supported the Patriot struggle for independence. Some people did not take sides. Some enslaved African Americans joined the British army because they hoped to earn their freedom. Many other people stayed loyal to Britain. These people were called Loyalists or Tories.

The Patriots did have some advantages, however. Their biggest advantage was having George Washington as their leader. The Patriots were fighting for their own freedom. They had a bigger stake in winning the war than did the **mercenaries,** or hired soldiers, who made up part of the British army. They were also fighting on their own land.

 **Notes** | **Read to Learn**

The Opposing Sides (continued)

Both local militia and the Continental Army fought for the Patriot cause. The Continental Congress established the Continental Army. However, Congress relied on the states to **recruit,** or enlist, soldiers. Soldiers usually signed up for one year. Some women also fought with the Patriot forces. For example, Molly Pitcher joined her husband in battle, and Deborah Sampson dressed as a boy in order to join the army.

Patriot Defeats and Victories (pages 156–158)

Finding the Main Idea

Circle the statement that best expresses the main idea of this section.

Important victories in New Jersey during the winter of 1776 gave the Patriots hope.

Washington asks Congress for more troops to defeat the British.

The Continental Army was badly outnumbered and suffered a defeat at the Battle of Long Island in August 1776. Despite defeat, Americans showed great bravery. Nathan Hale volunteered to spy on British troops and was hanged when he was discovered.

By the winter of 1776–1777, the Patriot cause looked lost. Supplies ran low. Many soldiers did not reenlist or they deserted. Washington badly needed more troops. He asked Congress to allow free African Americans to enlist. His request was met with resistance. Eventually, all states except South Carolina had African American soldiers. Lemuel Hayes and Peter Salem were two African Americans who fought at Concord.

During the cold winter, Washington saw a chance to catch the British off guard. On Christmas night 1776, he crossed the Delaware River with 2,400 troops. He surprised the British troops stationed at Trenton, New Jersey. His army marched on to Princeton, where they scored another victory. These victories gave hope to the Patriots.

A British Plan for Victory (pages 158–159)

Formulating Questions

Create a matching quiz using some of the key events and people described in this section. Exchange quizzes with a friend to test your knowledge.

The British planned a major attack in 1777 to take control of the Hudson River. The British wanted to separate New England from the Middle Colonies. The plan was that General John Burgoyne would lead a large force south from Canada. Lieutenant Colonel Barry St. Leger's troops would march east across New York from Lake Ontario. General Howe's troops would move north from New York City. They would meet at Albany and defeat the Patriot troops.

The plan failed for several reasons. First, Howe's troops captured Philadelphia. Washington responded by attacking the British at Germantown. Washington's attack slowed Howe's progress. Howe decided to stay in Philadelphia for the winter.

A British Plan for Victory (continued)

A Patriot force led by Benedict Arnold kept St. Leger from reaching Fort Stanwix, New York. Meanwhile, General Burgoyne captured Fort Ticonderoga in July. However, his progress south was slow, and he ran short on supplies. Burgoyne sent troops to attack the American supply base in Bennington, Vermont. A local militia, the Green Mountain Boys, defeated them. Burgoyne retreated to Saratoga, New York. American troops led by General Horatio Gates halted Burgoyne's progress. Burgoyne was forced to surrender at the Battle of Saratoga on October 17, 1777.

Section Wrap-Up

Answer these questions to check your understanding of the entire section.

1. **Contrasting** Contrast the British army and the Continental Army at the start of the war.

   _____

   _____

   _____

2. **Making Inferences** Why do you think Britain wanted to cut off New England from the rest of the colonies?

   _____

   _____

   _____

 **Informative Writing**

On a separate sheet of paper, describe the British plan for an attack in 1777. Discuss what happened, why it happened, and who was involved.

The War Continues

Essential Question

How did the United States gain allies and aid during the Revolutionary War?

Directions: As you read, complete a graphic organizer like the one below to list why France and Spain chose to support the Patriot cause and what support those countries offered.

	Reasons aid was offered	What was offered
France	1.	2.
Spain	3.	4.

 Notes | **Read to Learn**

Gaining Allies (pages 161–164)

Identifying Central Issues

Why was the Battle of Saratoga a turning point in the war?

_____

_____

_____

_____

_____

The Patriot victory in the Battle of Saratoga was a turning point in the war. France and other European nations realized that the Americans might win the war.

At Benjamin Franklin's urging, France secretly gave money to the Americans. After the Patriot victory, France announced its support for the United States and declared war on Britain. France sent money, supplies, and troops to help the Patriots.

Spain also declared war on Britain. Bernardo de Gálvez (GAHL•vez) was the Spanish governor of Louisiana. He led troops against Britain in the South. Gálvez's campaign kept some British troops away from other battles in the war. This indirectly helped the Patriots.

During the winter of 1777–1778, Howe's troops wintered in Philadelphia and Washington's troops wintered in Valley Forge, about 20 miles (32 km) away. The Continental Army did not have enough food, clothing, shelter, or medicine. It was a winter of terrible suffering. Many men **deserted,** or left the Continental Army without permission and some officers resigned.

 **Notes** | # Read to Learn

Gaining Allies (continued)

Defining

Use each vocabulary word in this section in a sentence:

1. deserted

_____

_____

2. inflation

_____

_____

_____

The Continental Army managed to survive the horrible winter. New soldiers joined in the spring. France's support of the Patriot cause boosted morale.

Several Europeans arrived in the United States to help the Patriots. The Marquis de Lafayette (LAH•fee•EHT), a French noble, became a trusted aide to Washington. Friedrich von Steuben (STOO•buhn), a former army officer from Prussia, also helped. He made the Patriot troops at Valley Forge better fighters. Juan de Miralles (mee•RAH•yays) from Spain helped raise money from Spain, Cuba, and Mexico.

Paying for the war continued to be a major problem. The Continental Congress could not raise money through taxes. The Congress printed hundreds of millions of dollars worth of paper money, but they did not have enough gold and silver to back up the money. This led to **inflation,** which meant that more and more paper money was needed to buy the same amount of goods. People quit using the paper money, but there was no other way to pay for the war.

Life on the Home Front (pages 164–165)

Paraphrasing

In your own words, describe why some people began to question slavery and the inequality of women.

_____

_____

_____

_____

The ideas of liberty and freedom inspired by the American Revolution gave some groups in American society hope that they, too, would win equality. Some women fought for women's rights. Judith Sargeant Murray argued that girls should get as good an education as boys. Abigail Adams protested to her husband, John Adams, about the power of husbands over wives.

Ideas of freedom also made some Americans question slavery. A few Northern states attempted to abolish slavery within their borders. Some African Americans fought on the Patriot side, hoping the Revolution would end slavery. However, slavery would continue for many years.

Many Loyalists left the colonies. Some Loyalists fought on the British side, or served as spies for the British. Those who remained after the war faced difficulties. Sometimes Loyalists were attacked by mobs. Loyalists who were suspected of helping the British could be arrested and tried as traitors.

Answer these questions to check your understanding of the entire section.

1. **Making Inferences** Why do you think France only gave the Patriots money and supplies in secret before the Battle of Saratoga?

_____

_____

2. **Drawing Conclusions** How did views of slavery change as a result of the American Revolution? What resulted?

_____

_____

In the space below, write a short description of the winter at Valley Forge from the point of view of a soldier in Washington's army.

_____

_____

_____

_____

_____

_____

_____

_____

_____

_____

_____

_____

_____

_____

The War Moves West and South

Essential Question

How did fighting in the West and South affect the course of the Revolutionary War?

Directions: As you read, complete a graphic organizer like the one below to list several victories of the British and the Patriots in the West and the South.

British Victories

1. _____
2. _____
3. _____

Patriot Victories

1. _____
2. _____
3. _____

 **Notes**   **Read to Learn**

War in the West (page 169)

Determining Cause and Effect

What strengthened the Americans' position in the West?

_____

_____

_____

Many Native Americans were concerned about losing their lands. Some Native Americans supported the Patriots. Others helped the British attack American settlements west of the Appalachian Mountains. Many of these attacks were brutal.

George Rogers Clark, an officer in the Virginia militia, set out to end British attacks in the West. In July 1778, his troops captured the British post at Kaskaskia (ka•SKAS•kee•uh) in present-day Illinois. Later they also captured the British town of Vincennes (vihn•SEHNZ) in present-day Indiana. After the British recaptured Vincennes, Clark attacked the British once again. He forced the British general Henry Hamilton to surrender. This strengthened the American position in the West.

Notes

Read to Learn

Glory at Sea (page 170)

Defining

What is a privateer?

_____

_____

The powerful ships of Britain's navy kept Patriot ships from entering and leaving American harbors. This **blockade** prevented supplies and troops from reaching the Continental Army.

The American navy was too weak to fight well against the British navy. Congress enlisted about 2,000 **privateers** to join the war effort. Privateers were privately owned and armed merchant ships. They captured more British ships at sea than the American navy did.

One American naval officer did have success against the British. John Paul Jones raided British ports. His ship defeated a British warship off the coast of Great Britain in September 1779. This victory made Jones a naval hero to American Patriots.

Struggles in the South (pages 171–173)

Finding the Main Idea

Circle the statement below that best expresses the main idea of this section.

• Because Nathanael Greene was a good commander, General Cornwallis was forced to abandon the Carolinas.

• The British waged a strong campaign in the South beginning in 1778 in the hopes that it would help win the war.

The British changed their strategy in 1778 as the war dragged on. They decided to concentrate on the South, where many Loyalists lived. In late 1778, British troops under Henry Clinton took Savannah, Georgia, and most of the state. The British also took the port city of Charles Town, South Carolina, in 1780.

General Charles Cornwallis commanded the British forces in the South. He could not control the area the British had captured, for several reasons. First, he did not receive much help from Loyalists. Second, small bands of Patriots used **guerrilla warfare** to weaken the British forces. In guerrilla warfare, small bands of soldiers launched sudden attacks and then disappeared again. Francis Marion was a successful guerrilla leader whom the British could not catch.

The Spanish governor of Louisiana, Bernardo de Gálvez, also helped the colonists in the war effort. He lent the Patriots money and opened the New Orleans port to American trade. He sent supplies and ammunition up the Mississippi River as well. After Spain declared war on Britain in 1779, Gálvez raised an army and captured several British posts along the lower Mississippi.

The Patriots forced a British retreat in the Carolinas in September 1780. Afterward, Southern support for the Patriot cause grew. Continental forces commanded by Nathanael Greene defeated the British at Cowpens, South Carolina. Later, Greene's troops forced General Cornwallis to abandon the Carolinas and march north to Virginia. Cornwallis set up camp at Yorktown, Virginia. In the meantime, General Washington sent troops south to join the fight against Cornwallis.

Section Wrap-Up

Answer these questions to check your understanding of the entire section.

1. **Making Inferences** Why do you think Native Americans joined with the British to attack American settlements west of the Appalachian Mountains?

   _____

   _____

2. **Comparing and Contrasting** Compare and contrast the contributions of the American navy and privateers to the war effort.

   _____

   _____

In the space below, write an essay explaining why the British strategy in the South did not work. Use facts from the reading to support your point of view.

   _____

   _____

   _____

   _____

   _____

   _____

   _____

   _____

   _____

   _____

   _____

   _____

Chapter 6, Section 4 (Pages 174–178)

The War Is Won

Essential Question

How did the Battle of Yorktown lead to American independence?

Directions: As you read, complete the cause-and-effect diagram below showing the effects of trapping Cornwallis in Yorktown.

| Combined American and French forces trap Cornwallis at Yorktown. | → | | → | |

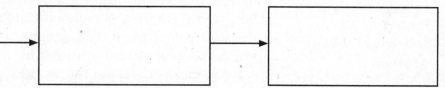

Victory at Yorktown *(pages 175–176)*

Determining Cause and Effect

Why did George Washington change his plan to attack British troops in New York City?

_____

_____

_____

_____

_____

General George Washington planned to attack the British when French forces arrived. French warships landed at Newport, Rhode Island, in July 1780. They carried soldiers commanded by Comte de Rochambeau (ROH•SHAM•BOH). However, the British fleet trapped the French ships in the harbor. Washington waited for a second fleet of French ships to arrive. He was counting on their support to attack General Clinton's army based in New York City.

When Washington learned the French navy ships were headed toward the Chesapeake Bay, he changed his plans. He would attack British forces in Yorktown, Virginia, rather than in New York City. He was joined by Rochambeau and his troops in July 1781. The combined troops marched south toward Virginia. They joined Lafayette's troops to attack the British. Cornwallis's troops were now outnumbered. A French fleet kept British forces from escaping by sea.

The Americans and French began bombarding the British in Yorktown on October 9. Ten days later, Cornwallis surrendered. The Patriots had won the Battle of Yorktown.

The Patriot victory at Yorktown was a turning point in the war. The British decided that it was too costly to continue. Representatives from both countries met in Paris to work out a treaty. Benjamin Franklin, John Adams, and John Jay represented the United States. The Treaty of Paris was **ratified,** or approved, by Congress in April 1783. It was signed on September 3, 1783. The British recognized the United States as an independent nation.

Read to Learn

Independence (pages 177–178)

Distinguishing Fact From Opinion

Circle the statements below that are fact. Underline the statements that are opinion.

1. The British recognized the United States as an independent nation.

2. The patriotic spirit of the American people was an important reason they won the war.

3. Americans knew how to lay an ambush.

4. Freedom and equality are ideals worth fighting for.

5. Saint Domingue won independence from colonial rule in 1804.

The Continental Army was stationed in Newburgh, New York, after the British surrender. Congress refused to pay the soldiers or provide them with pensions. The soldiers grew angry. Officers wrote a letter threatening to attack Congress if their demands were not met. George Washington recognized the danger of a revolt from the troops. He convinced the soldiers to be patient. He then persuaded Congress to meet the soldiers' demand for payment. The danger of a revolt ended. Washington retired soon after and returned home to Mount Vernon, Virginia.

Americans defeated the world's greatest power for several reasons. Americans fought on their own land. The British had to bring soldiers and supplies from thousands of miles away. The British depended heavily on their navy. When their ships were blocked, British troops had no support. Americans knew how and where to lay an **ambush,** or a surprise attack. Help from other nations contributed to the American victory. Most importantly, the American Revolution was supported by the American people. The Patriots were determined to win.

The ideas of the Declaration of Independence influenced others. French rebels embraced the ideas of freedom and equality beginning in 1789. Then, in 1791, enslaved Africans in the French colony of Saint Domingue fought to win their freedom. In 1804 Saint Domingue became the second nation in the Americas to win independence from colonial rule.

Section Wrap-Up

Answer these questions to check your understanding of the entire section.

1. **Analyzing** Why were French and American troops able to force Cornwallis to surrender quickly?

   _____

   _____

2. **Making Generalizations** How did the American Revolution affect the rest of the world?

   _____

   _____

In the space below, write an essay explaining the reasons why Americans were able to win their independence from the strongest military power in the world.

_____

_____

_____

_____

_____

_____

_____

_____

_____

_____

_____

_____

_____

_____

The Articles of Confederation

Essential Question

How effective was government under the Articles of Confederation?

Directions: As you read, complete a graphic organizer like the one below to identify the powers that the national government had under the Articles of Confederation.

1. _____ 2. _____ → **Powers of the national government under the Articles** → 3. _____ 4. _____

 **Notes** | **Read to Learn**

From Independent States to a Republic (pages 187–189)

Specifying

Circle the letter that best answers the question.

Under the Articles of Confederation, who would have been allowed to vote?

A. an enslaved person in the South

B. a 25-year-old white, male landowner

C. a 30-year-old white woman

D. an 18-year-old male servant

In May 1776, the Second Continental Congress asked states to organize their governments. Each state adopted a **constitution,** or plan of government. States adopted constitutions that limited the powers of governors. They also divided duties between the governor and the legislature. Most states set up a **bicameral,** or two-house, legislature. States wanted the people to have power. They gave people the right to vote for legislators. In most states, voters had to be white males who were at least 21 years old. They also had to own land or pay a certain amount of taxes.

Americans wanted the United States to be a republic. A **republic** is a government in which citizens rule through elected representatives. Most Americans wanted a weak central government. They expected that states would act like small countries.

In 1777 Congress adopted the Articles of Confederation, America's first constitution. Under the Articles, Congress could conduct foreign affairs, issue currency, borrow money, and maintain the armed forces. Congress could not impose taxes, force citizens to join the army, or regulate trade. States would keep most of their power. The states approved the Articles, and the Confederation became the government of the United States on March 1, 1781.

Read to Learn

New Land Policies (pages 190–191)

Making Inferences

How do you think the settlers felt about land speculators? Why?

_____

_____

_____

_____

_____

During the late 1700s, more people began moving west. These settlers hoped to organize their lands as states. The central government took control of western lands and divided them into districts. These districts could then apply, or **petition,** for statehood when their populations increased.

In 1785 Congress passed an **ordinance,** or law, to sell western lands north of the Ohio River. This law divided the land to sell at auction. Land speculators hoped to use the law to buy large amounts of land cheaply.

Congress passed the Northwest Ordinance in 1787 to protect the property rights of settlers. This ordinance created the Northwest Territory, which was divided into smaller territories. When the population of a smaller territory reached 60,000, it could apply to become a state. The new states would grant the same rights as the original states. Slavery was not allowed.

Trouble on Two Fronts (pages 191–193)

Determining Cause and Effect

Complete the following sentence:

The British refused to talk to John Adams because the United States had not paid

_____ *for*

_____

_____ .

By 1781, the United States had money problems. The money printed during the Revolutionary War had **depreciated,** or fallen in value. The Continental Congress and the states both printed money, but they had no gold or silver to back it up. The money was almost worthless. The cost of food and other goods rose. The government still owed a large debt from the Revolutionary War. It could not pay its debts because it had no power to tax.

To help solve the money problems, Congress tried to change the Articles of Confederation so it could tax imports. Though 12 of 13 states approved the plan, the opposition of Rhode Island killed it. The financial crisis got worse.

The United States began having problems with Britain. The British had not honored their promise to leave the lands east of the Mississippi River. American merchants also claimed that Britain was keeping them out of the West Indies and other markets. The United States sent John Adams to Britain to discuss the problems. The British refused to talk. They said that the United States had not kept its promise to pay Loyalists for land taken from them during the Revolutionary War. Congress did not have the power to require the states to pay.

Trouble on Two Fronts (continued)

Relations between the United States and Spain were even worse. Spain controlled Florida and lands west of the Mississippi River. Spain did not want the United States to expand into its territory. To keep Americans out, Spain closed the lower part of the Mississippi River. Now Western settlers could not use the river to ship their goods. Many Americans began to agree that the central government needed more power to handle the country's problems.

Section Wrap-Up

Answer these questions to check your understanding of the entire section.

1. **Identifying Central Issues** The title of the last section is "Trouble on Two Fronts." What are the "two fronts" discussed in the section?

_____

_____

2. **Making Inferences** Why do you think the central government had trouble getting the states to give it the right to impose import taxes?

_____

_____

 **Expository Writing**

In the space below, write a letter to the Spanish government suggesting a solution to the blockade of the Mississippi River. Be sure to mention how Spain would benefit if the river were opened to American ships.

_____

_____

_____

_____

_____

_____

Chapter 7, Section 2 (Pages 194–201)

Convention and Compromise

Essential Question

Why is the Constitution a document of compromise?

Directions: As you read, complete a graphic organizer like the one below to understand the positions of the Northern and Southern states on slavery.

Slavery Issues	
Counting Enslaved People	**Slavery**
1. North: _____ _____	1. North: _____ _____
2. South: _____ _____	2. South: _____ _____

Read to Learn

A Call for Change (pages 195–197)

Determining Cause and Effect

Why did the government take farmers' land?

_____
_____
_____
_____
_____

After the Revolutionary War, the United States suffered a depression. A **depression** is a time when the economy slows and unemployment increases. Farmers could not sell their goods and could not give the government money to pay war debts. The government put some farmers in jail and took farmers' land.

Daniel Shays led a group of angry farmers to the federal arsenal to take weapons. The state militia put down the uprising. Shays's Rebellion caused many Americans to worry that the government was weak.

In the late 1700s, the states were divided on the issue of slavery. Many states taxed or outlawed the slave trade. The first antislavery group was organized in the North in 1774. Northern states began to free enslaved people.

Southern states kept slavery legal. However, some farmers began freeing enslaved people. A law in Virginia encouraged **manumission,** or the freeing of the state's enslaved people.

The Constitutional Convention (pages 197–199)

Naming

Who led the meeting in Philadelphia?

_____

_____

Some American leaders were unhappy with the Articles of Confederation. They called for change. Fifty-five delegates met in Philadelphia in May 1787 to consider changes to the Articles. The delegates chose George Washington to lead the meetings.

The delegates from Virginia gave a plan for a strong central government. There would be a court system, a two-house legislature, and a chief executive chosen by the legislature. The lower house would be elected by the people. The upper house would be chosen by the lower house. In both houses, the number of representatives would correspond in size, or be **proportional,** to the population of each state.

The delegates from New Jersey were worried about the states with smaller populations. These states would lose power under the Virginia Plan. The New Jersey delegates only wanted to revise the Articles. They did not want to write a new constitution. The New Jersey Plan had a legislature with one house. Each state would continue to get one vote. Congress would elect a weak executive branch. The New Jersey Plan also would allow Congress to collect taxes and regulate trade.

Compromise Wins Out (pages 200–201)

Calculating

Solve the following problem:

Assume that 8,500 enslaved people live in a state. These enslaved people would count as how many free people for the purpose of representation?

A. 4,250 people

B. 5,100 people

C. 5,525 people

D. 6,750 people

The delegates decided to write a constitution for a new government. They agreed upon what became known as the Great Compromise. A **compromise** is an agreement between two or more sides. In a compromise, each side usually gives up something it wants.

The delegates decided on a two-house legislature. The number of seats in the lower house would vary depending on a state's population. For the upper house, each state would have two seats.

The delegates compromised on how to count enslaved people. This count was for the purpose of taxation and representation. The Southern states wanted to count enslaved people in their population. The Northern delegates did not agree because enslaved people were thought of as property. The delegates decided to count each enslaved person as three-fifths of a free person. That would mean that every five enslaved people would count as three free people. Enslaved people, however, were not given the right to vote.

Northern states also wanted to ban slavery nationwide. The South opposed this plan because they thought that would hurt their economy. Northern delegates feared that Southern states

Compromise Wins Out (continued)

might leave the nation over slavery. The delegates decided to leave the issue of slavery alone until 1808.

Delegates also wanted a bill of rights. They thought a bill of rights would keep the national government from abusing its power. Most delegates did not think a bill of rights was necessary. On September 17, 1787, all but three delegates approved the Constitution.

Section Wrap-Up

Answer these questions to check your understanding of the entire section.

1. **Predicting** Why did the delegates put off the slavery issue when writing the new constitution? Would this issue be easier to settle in the future? Explain.

_____

_____

2. **Identifying Points of View** What were the delegates' arguments for and against including a bill of rights in the Constitution?

_____

_____

**Informative Writing**

In the space below, write a letter to a friend describing the major issues at the Constitutional Convention. Be sure to include only facts, not your opinions.

_____

_____

_____

_____

_____

_____

A New Plan of Government

Essential Question

What ideas and features are found in the United States Constitution?

Directions: As you read, complete a graphic organizer like the one below to identify the ideas and features in the United States Constitution.

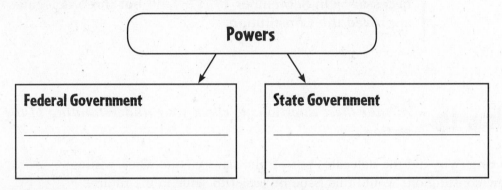

Powers

Federal Government

State Government

Notes

Read to Learn

Roots of the Constitution (pages 205–207)

Organizing

Complete the outline:

I. Magna Carta
A. Limited power of king
*B.*_____

II. European writers
A. Locke:

_____

B. Montesquieu:
Believed in limited, separated, balanced powers

The Framers of the Constitution were influenced by British ideas and traditions. They kept European ideas in mind as they wrote the Constitution.

One influence on the Constitution was the Magna Carta. This document limited the power of the English king. It created Parliament, England's lawmaking body. England had a bill of rights. Many delegates felt that Americans needed a bill of rights.

The ideas of some European writers were important to the delegates. The English writer John Locke believed that people have natural rights. These include the right to life, liberty, and property. The French writer Baron de Montesquieu also had important ideas. He thought that the powers of government should be limited, separated, and balanced against each other. This would keep one person or group from becoming too powerful.

The states held most of the power under the Articles of Confederation. This changed under the Constitution. The Constitution created a federalist system. **Federalism** is the sharing of power between the federal and state governments. The federal government could impose taxes, regulate trade, control the currency, raise an army, and declare war. It could also create new

 **Notes** | # Read to Learn

Roots of the Constitution (continued)

laws. The state governments kept many important powers. The states could regulate trade within their borders, establish local governments and schools, and set marriage and divorce laws.

The federal government and the states would also share some powers. These include the power to tax and to enforce laws. The Constitution became the supreme law of the land. No state could make laws that went against the Constitution.

The New Government (pages 207–208)

Contrasting

Fill in the blanks below:

1. The legislative branch _____ laws.

2. The executive branch _____ laws.

The Framers of the Constitution divided the federal government into three branches. The **legislative branch,** or Congress, is the lawmaking branch. Congress includes a House of Representatives and a Senate. The number of members in each house was decided in the Great Compromise. The legislative branch has the power to make laws, coin money, collect taxes, and regulate trade.

An **executive branch** carries out the nation's laws. The president is in charge of this branch. He is elected by the **Electoral College,** or presidential electors. The president is chief of the armed forces and conducts relations with foreign countries.

The Framers also created a **judicial branch,** or court system. These courts hear cases involving the Constitution, laws passed by Congress, and disputes between states.

To limit, or check, the power of each branch, the Framers included a system of **checks and balances.** For example, both houses of Congress must pass a bill before it can become law. The president can veto, or reject, the laws of Congress. Supreme Court judges are appointed by the president but must be approved by the Senate. The Supreme Court checks Congress by making sure that laws do not conflict with the Constitution.

Debate and Adoption (pages 209–210)

Differentiating

Circle the name of the group you believe had the best argument.

- *Federalists*

- *Anti-Federalists*

The Constitution was given to the states for their approval. For the Constitution to go into effect, nine states had to approve it. People throughout the country debated the Constitution.

Supporters of the new Constitution were called Federalists. Federalist leaders wrote essays defending the Constitution. These essays are called the Federalist Papers.

Those who opposed the Constitution were called Anti-Federalists. They also wrote essays to support their beliefs. These papers were called the Anti-Federalist Papers.

Debate and Adoption (continued)

Anti-Federalists feared the national government would favor wealthy people. They thought it might take away people's liberties. They preferred local governments that the people could directly control. Anti-Federalists wanted a bill of rights **amendment,** or addition, to the Constitution.

By June 21, 1788, nine states had approved the Constitution. But the two most populous states, New York and Virginia, had not approved it. Virginia approved the Constitution after being promised that a bill of rights amendment would be added. By 1790, all states had approved the Constitution.

Section Wrap-Up

Answer these questions to check your understanding of the entire section.

1. **Explaining** Explain the system of checks and balances in the Constitution.

_____

_____

2. **Making Inferences** By June 21, 1788, enough states had ratified the Constitution for it to be put into effect. Why did the Framers agree to include the Bill of Rights?

_____

_____

 **Persuasive Writing**

In the space below, write a letter explaining why a bill of rights is necessary for the Constitution. Include historical evidence to support your argument.

_____

_____

_____

_____

_____

The First President

Essential Question

What were the precedents that Washington established as the first president of the United States?

Directions: As you read, complete a graphic organizer like the one below to identify the cabinet created by Washington.

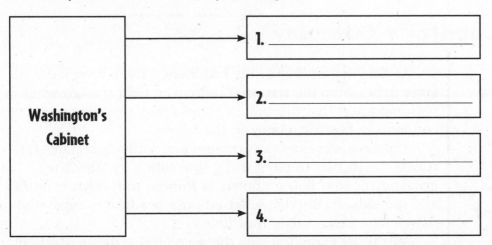

Washington's Cabinet

1. _____

2. _____

3. _____

4. _____

Notes

Read to Learn

President Washington (pages 253–255)

Classifying

Circle the cabinet department that would deal with tax collection.

Department of the Treasury

Department of War

State Department

George Washington became president on April 30, 1789. John Adams became vice president. As the first president, Washington expected to set **precedents,** or traditions. These precedents would shape the future of the United States.

Congress set up three departments in the executive branch. The State Department dealt with other countries. The Department of the Treasury took care of money matters. The Department of War handled the country's defense. The attorney general took care of the country's legal affairs. The heads of these three departments and the attorney general became known as the **cabinet.** The president was given the power to dismiss cabinet officials.

With the Judiciary Act of 1789, Congress created a federal court system. This system had 13 district courts and three circuit courts. The federal courts could reverse the decisions of state courts. The Supreme Court would be the final authority on many issues. A chief justice was approved as head of the Supreme Court.

Americans feared that a strong central government would not respect individual rights. Many states had supported the

Read to Learn

President Washington *(continued)*

Constitution because they were promised a bill of rights. To protect civil rights, Congress proposed 12 amendments to the Constitution. The states approved 10 of the amendments in December 1791. These amendments are known as the Bill of Rights. The Bill of Rights protects individual liberties. These include the right of free speech and the right of trial by jury.

The New Country's Economy *(pages 255–257)*

Formulating Questions

As you read, ask yourself questions to make sure you understand the text. Remember the 5 Ws when you think of questions—who, what, when, where, and why. Use one of these words to write one question and answer about this passage in the space below.

_____

_____

_____

_____

_____

Identifying

Underline the names of the two people who did not want a national bank.

As Washington began his presidency, the nation faced a large debt called the **national debt.** The debt was growing. It was important that the United States repay this debt so it could continue to borrow money in the future.

The Confederation government and individual states borrowed the money to pay for the Revolutionary War. The government sold notes, known as **bonds,** to foreign countries and individuals. Bonds are based on a promise to repay the money in a certain length of time.

Alexander Hamilton was the secretary of the treasury. In 1790 he suggested that the new federal government pay the debts owed to other countries and individuals. Congress agreed to pay other countries. There was protest over paying the debt to individuals. Many people who originally bought bonds later sold them to speculators for less than the purchase price. Hamilton wanted the bonds to be repaid at the original price. Critics of Hamilton's plan thought this would make speculators rich. The original bond purchasers felt betrayed.

Hamilton also proposed that the federal government assume all the war debts of the states. Southern states complained that this deal was unfair. They thought they would have to pay more than their share. Hamilton worked out a compromise with Southern leaders. He agreed to locate the nation's capital between Virginia and Maryland in a district called Washington, D.C. In return, he got support from the Southern states for his financial plan.

To help build a strong economy, Hamilton also asked Congress to create a national bank. James Madison and Thomas Jefferson believed a national bank would be **unconstitutional,** or inconsistent with the Constitution. Washington agreed with Hamilton, however. In 1792 a national bank was established.

Hamilton believed America would benefit from more manufacturing. He proposed a tariff to protect new American industries. A **tariff** is a tax on imports. The South disapproved of the tariff because the region had little industry. Congress supported the tariff.

The New Country's Economy (continued)

Analyzing

Why did the South not support a tariff?

_____

_____

_____

Hamilton also proposed a national tax to help pay off the country's debt. He wanted to give the federal government new financial powers. Some leaders opposed this idea. These opponents thought Hamilton's plan would help the wealthy control the national government.

Section Wrap-Up

Answer these questions to check your understanding of the entire section.

1. **Explaining** How could speculators profit from Hamilton's plan to settle the national debt?

_____

_____

2. **Analyzing** How would a tariff benefit the American economy?

_____

_____

Persuasive Writing

In the space below, write a letter from Alexander Hamilton to the American people. In the letter, ask for support of your plan to settle the nation's debts and provide arguments that support it.

_____

_____

_____

_____

_____

_____

_____

_____

_____

Early Challenges

Essential Question

What challenges did the United States face during Washington's administration?

Directions: As you read, complete a graphic organizer like the one below to summarize the effects of three major treaties of Washington's presidency.

Treaty		Effect
Treaty of Greenville	⟹	1. _____
Jay's Treaty	⟹	2. _____
Pinckney's Treaty	⟹	3. _____

Notes

Read to Learn

The Whiskey Rebellion and the West (pages 261–262)

Defining

What is a rebellion?

_____

_____

Specifying

Circle the event that took place in 1794.

Battle of Fallen Timbers

Whiskey Rebellion

Treaty of Greenville

In 1791 Congress taxed the making and selling of whiskey. This tax angered farmers in western Pennsylvania. In July 1794, they attacked the tax collectors. They burned buildings. This uprising was called the Whiskey Rebellion. It alarmed national leaders. Washington sent a force to put down the rebellion. This sent a message to citizens. The government would use force to keep order.

Problems also occurred in the West. Washington worried about the European powers there. He signed treaties with the Native Americans. Washington hoped these treaties would lessen the influence of the British and Spanish on the Native Americans. American settlers acted against the treaties. They settled on Native American lands. Fighting broke out between American settlers and Native Americans.

Washington sent an army to the West. It was led by General Arthur St. Clair. In November 1791, the Native Americans defeated St. Clair's army. The Native Americans said all settlers should leave lands north of the Ohio River.

Some Americans wanted France as an ally in the West. They thought the French could help defeat the British, Spanish, and Native Americans. The British reacted by asking

Copyright © Glencoe/McGraw-Hill, a division of The McGraw-Hill Companies, Inc.

 **Notes** | **Read to Learn**

The Whiskey Rebellion and the West (continued)

Native Americans to attack American settlements. The British also began to build a new fort.

Washington sent another army to the West. It was led by Anthony Wayne. In August 1794, this army defeated the Native Americans at the Battle of Fallen Timbers. Native Americans had to give up their lands. The Native Americans signed the Treaty of Greenville. In this treaty, they surrendered most of their lands in what is now Ohio.

Problems With Europe (pages 262–263)

Distinguishing Fact From Opinion

Circle the letter of the statement below that is an opinion.

A. Neutral countries do not take sides.

B. A policy of neutrality is best.

C. Washington kept Americans from fighting for the British.

In 1793 Britain and France went to war. Some Americans supported Britain, while others supported France. Washington supported a policy of **neutrality** for the United States. This meant the United States would not take sides in the war.

France tried to involve the United States in its fight with Britain. The French tried to get Americans to attack British ships. Washington issued a Proclamation of Neutrality. This said that Americans could not fight in the war. It also said French and British warships could not come into American ports.

The British captured American ships that traded with the French. They forced the American sailors on these ships to be part of the British navy. This was known as **impressment.** It angered Americans.

Washington wanted a peaceful solution. He sent John Jay to talk with Britain. John Jay was the chief justice of the Supreme Court. In Jay's Treaty, the British agreed to leave American lands. Most Americans did not like the treaty. The treaty did not deal with impressment. It did not deal with the British interruption of American trade. But the treaty ended the conflict.

Spanish leaders worried that the British and Americans would work together against Spain. Thomas Pinckney talked to Spanish leaders. In 1795 Spain and the United States signed Pinckney's Treaty. This treaty allowed Americans to travel the Mississippi River and trade in New Orleans.

After two terms in office, Washington decided to leave his job as president. In his farewell address, he said he still believed in neutrality. He said Americans should be careful about alliances with other countries. His words influenced the nation's foreign policy for more than 100 years.

 **Answer these questions to check your understanding of the entire section.**

1. **Predicting** How would the Treaty of Greenville affect the nation's future?

   _____

   _____

2. **Evaluating** Why was Jay's Treaty criticized?

   _____

   _____

 *In the space below, write a diary entry from Washington's point of view. In the diary entry, discuss the advantages of fighting the Native Americans in Ohio.*

_____

_____

_____

_____

_____

_____

_____

_____

_____

The First Political Parties

Essential Question

How did the Federalist and Republican Parties form, and on what issues did they disagree?

Directions: As you read, complete a graphic organizer like the one below to identify the major differences between Federalists and Republicans regarding the role of the federal government.

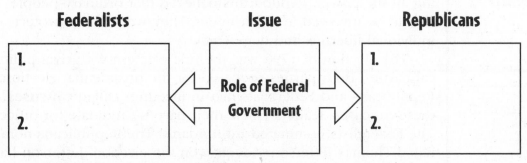

Federalists   Issue   Republicans

1.

2.

Role of Federal Government

1.

2.

Notes   **Read to Learn**

Opposing Views (pages 265–268)

Naming

Circle the groups of people who supported the Federalist Party.

small farmers

urban workers

Republican leaders

wealthy plantation owners

Most Americans admired Washington. However, some Americans did not like his policies. Most of these people supported Thomas Jefferson. In Washington's cabinet, Alexander Hamilton and Thomas Jefferson often disagreed. Washington most often supported Hamilton's views.

Most Americans were **partisan,** meaning they favored one side of an issue. By 1796, two political parties had formed. These two parties disagreed about the role of the federal government.

The Federalists wanted a strong federal government. This party believed in a government with implied powers. **Implied powers** are powers that are not forbidden by the Constitution. Federalist policies favored banking and shipping interests. Their strongest supporters were wealthy plantation owners and Americans in the Northeast. Hamilton was a Federalist.

Thomas Jefferson and James Madison organized a party that disagreed with Hamilton. Members of this party were called the Republicans or Democratic-Republicans. Republicans thought the federal government should have only those powers specifically given to it by the Constitution. This meant the central government had limited powers. Small farmers and urban workers, especially those in the South, agreed.

Opposing Views (continued)

Copyright © Glencoe/McGraw-Hill, a division of The McGraw-Hill Companies, Inc.

Identifying Points of View

The Federalists and Republicans disagreed on what two main points?

_____

_____

_____

_____

Federalists thought that too much democracy was not a good thing. They believed people should be represented by honest, educated men who owned property. These people could best protect individual liberties. They believed that ordinary people were not dependable and had poor judgment, and that their views could be easily swayed.

Republicans did not like the idea of just a few people having all the power. Republicans believed that ordinary people should be involved in government. They would help protect individual liberties and democracy.

The election of 1796 was the first election with rival political parties. Both parties prepared for the presidential election. Republicans and Federalists met in meetings called **caucuses.** In these caucuses, leaders chose their party's candidate for office. The Federalists nominated John Adams. The Republicans nominated Thomas Jefferson. Adams won the election. Jefferson had the next-greatest number of electoral votes. According to the Constitution at that time, Jefferson was made vice president.

President John Adams (pages 269–270)

Drawing Conclusions

Complete the following sentence:

After being told about the French agents, Adams felt

_____.

Write the sentence from the text that led you to this conclusion.

_____

_____

_____

_____

France resented the agreement the United States had made with Britain called Jay's Treaty. France began to seize American ships taking goods to Britain. In 1797 Adams sent officials to France to discuss the problem. The French foreign minister would not meet with them. Instead, he sent French agents to the meeting. They demanded a bribe and asked for a loan for France. The Americans refused and told Adams about the meeting. Adams spoke with Congress. He named the French agents X, Y, and Z. He told Congress to prepare for war with France. This event was named the XYZ Affair.

Americans felt anger toward France. They began to distrust aliens. **Aliens** are immigrants living in the country who are not citizens. Americans thought some aliens would not be loyal to the United States during a possible war with France. Federalists passed the Alien and Sedition Acts. **Sedition** is an act aimed at weakening the government. The Alien Act allowed the government to put aliens in jail or send them out of the country.

Republicans disagreed with the Federalists. They thought these acts were unconstitutional. They responded with the Virginia and Kentucky Resolutions. In these papers, the Republicans said the Alien and Sedition Acts were unconstitutional. The Kentucky

President John Adams (continued)

Resolutions proposed that the states nullify federal laws that were unconstitutional. To **nullify** an act is to legally overturn it.

The resolutions supported the idea of **states' rights.** Under this idea, the federal government should have only those powers clearly given to it in the Constitution. The states should have all the powers not clearly forbidden to them.

The Federalists asked Adams to declare war on France, but he refused. Instead, he sent officials to France again. In 1800 the French agreed to a treaty. The Federalists were not happy with Adams, however. The Federalist Party began to split.

Section Wrap-Up

Answer these questions to check your understanding of the entire section.

1. **Drawing Conclusions** According to the Federalists, why would it be difficult for ordinary people to be effective in governing the nation?

_____

_____

2. **Identifying Central Issues** Why did the Republicans protest the Alien and Sedition Acts through the states of Kentucky and Virginia?

_____

_____

Informative Writing

In the space below, write a report for Congress detailing the XYZ Affair. Write from the point of view of one of the American delegates at the meeting.

_____

_____

_____

_____

_____

_____

The Republicans Take Power

Essential Question

In what ways did Thomas Jefferson and the Republicans limit the powers of the government?

Directions: As you read, complete a graphic organizer like the one below to show how Thomas Jefferson and the Republicans limited the powers of the federal government.

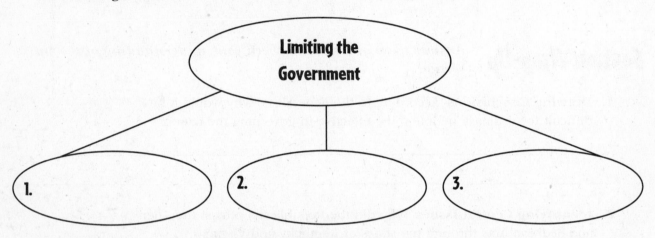

 **Notes**

Read to Learn

The Election of 1800 *(pages 277–278)*

Identifying Points of View

How did Jefferson think the government should be run?

_____

_____

_____

_____

In the 1800 election, Republicans nominated Thomas Jefferson and Aaron Burr for president and vice president. Federalists supported President John Adams and his running mate, Charles Pinckney. When members of the Electoral College voted, Jefferson and Burr each received 73 electoral votes. At the time, the electors chose both the president and the vice president in a single election. The person with the most votes would become president and the runner-up would become vice president. This made tie votes possible.

To break the tie, the House of Representatives had to decide the election. After many tied votes in the House, Jefferson became president and Burr become vice president. In 1803 the Twelfth Amendment was passed to prevent future ties between a presidential and vice-presidential candidate. Electors were required to cast a separate vote for each position.

The Election of 1800 (continued)

In his Inaugural Address, Jefferson listed his goals. He hoped for a government that would make wise choices, spend money carefully, and support the rights of state governments. Jefferson believed in reducing the power and size of government. His ideas were like the French philosophy of **laissez-faire** (LEH•SAY FEHR). This means "let [people] do [as they choose]."

Jefferson's Presidency (pages 278–279)

Analyzing

Why did Jefferson reduce the number of government workers?

_____

_____

_____

With the help of Albert Gallatin, secretary of the treasury, Jefferson reduced the national debt. He cut military spending. He also repealed all federal internal taxes. The government would get money only from the sale of western lands and from **customs duties.** Customs duties are taxes on imported goods. Jefferson also reduced the number of federal government workers to a few hundred people.

At the end of John Adams's presidency, the Federalists passed the Judiciary Act of 1801. This act set up regional courts for the United States with 16 judges and other officials. In his last days as president, Adams assigned hundreds of people to these positions. He also asked John Marshall, secretary of state, to act as chief justice. Adams made these appointments before he left office to make sure that Federalists, not Republicans, would control the courts.

Adams and Marshall tried to process all of these appointments before Adams left office. However, a few were not delivered in time. When Jefferson took over as president, he stopped some of these appointments, including one for William Marbury. Marbury tried to force his appointment by taking his case to the Supreme Court.

In *Marbury* v. *Madison,* John Marshall turned down Marbury's case. He said that the Constitution did not give the Supreme Court power to decide the case. The case established three principles of **judicial review.** First, the Constitution is the supreme law. Second, the Constitution must be followed when there is a disagreement between it and any other law. Third, the judicial branch must uphold the Constitution and cancel unconstitutional laws.

Under Marshall, the Supreme Court increased federal power. In *McCulloch* v. *Maryland,* the Court decided that Congress is allowed to do more than the Constitution specifically states it may do. In *Gibbons* v. *Ogden,* the Court decided that federal law had priority over state laws in interstate transportation.

Section Wrap-Up

Answer these questions to check your understanding of the entire section.

1. **Analyzing** Why did a tie occur in the Electoral College in the 1800 election? Could such a tie happen today in the College? Explain.

_____

_____

_____

_____

2. **Predicting** Why did Adams assign so many judges in his last days as president? How did he think the court would be different if the next president were to make the appointments?

_____

_____

_____

_____

In the space provided, write an essay explaining why the case of Marbury v. Madison *was so significant.*

_____

_____

_____

_____

_____

_____

_____

_____

_____

_____

_____

_____

The Louisiana Purchase

Essential Question

How did the Louisiana Purchase affect the nation's economy and politics?

Directions: As you read, complete a chart like the one below to explain how the Louisiana Purchase affected the nation's economy and politics.

Effects of the Louisiana Purchase	
1. Economy	2. Politics

 **Notes**

Read to Learn

Western Territory *(pages 281–282)*

Speculating

Why did settlers carry guns and axes on their journey?

_____

_____

_____

In the early 1800s, American settlers filled **Conestoga wagons** with guns, axes, and other belongings and headed west to look for land and adventure. Conestoga wagons were sturdy vehicles topped with white canvas.

In 1800 the territory of the United States went only as far west as the Mississippi River. The area to the west of the river was known as the Louisiana Territory. It was owned by Spain. New Orleans was on the southern edge of the territory. Spain allowed Americans to sail on the lower part of the Mississippi River and trade in New Orleans. This agreement was vital so that western farmers could ship their crops to markets.

In 1802 Spain changed its policy and no longer allowed American goods to move into or out of New Orleans. Jefferson learned that Spain and France had made a secret agreement to hand over the Louisiana Territory to France. Jefferson was afraid that France might stop American trade on the Mississippi River. He authorized the minister to France to offer as much as $10 million for New Orleans and West Florida.

The Nation Expands (pages 283–285)

Identifying

What were three goals of the Lewis and Clark expedition?

1. _____

2. _____

3. _____

Summarizing

What were the results of Lewis and Clark's expedition?

_____

_____

_____

France's leader, Napoleon Bonaparte, had plans to build an empire in the Americas. It would be based in Santo Domingo, which is now Haiti. But rebels took control of Santo Domingo, and Napoleon gave up his plans. France needed money to pay for a war with Britain. Napoleon offered to sell the entire Louisiana Territory to the United States. The purchase would provide cheap land for farmers and would give the United States control of the Mississippi River. The purchase of the territory was approved in 1803. It cost $15 million and doubled the size of the United States.

Jefferson convinced Congress to pay for an expedition to explore the Louisiana Territory. He wanted to learn about plants and animals there and find locations for forts. He also hoped to find the fabled "Northwest Passage" that would allow a more direct route to Asia.

Meriwether Lewis and William Clark were hired to lead the expedition. Both were amateur scientists who had experience with Native Americans. They assembled a crew of expert river men, scouts, gunsmiths, carpenters, a cook, and two interpreters. The expedition left St. Louis in the spring of 1804. Along the way, a Shoshone woman, Sacagawea, joined their group as a guide.

After 18 months and almost 4,000 miles (6,437.4 km), the group reached the Pacific Ocean. They had collected important information about the people, plants, animals, and geography of the West. Their journey inspired people to move westward.

Lieutenant Zebulon Pike led two more expeditions. He explored the upper Mississippi River valley and present-day Colorado. He found the mountain now known as Pikes Peak. He also explored the Great Plains, the Rocky Mountains, the Rio Grande, and what is now southern Texas.

Many Federalists were against the Louisiana Purchase. They were afraid that new states that developed in the territory would become Republican. A group of Federalists in Massachusetts planned to **secede,** or withdraw from the Union. They knew that they needed New York's support. They turned to Aaron Burr for help.

Alexander Hamilton accused Burr of plotting treason. When Burr lost the governor's race in New York, he blamed Hamilton. He challenged Hamilton to a duel. During the duel, Burr shot Hamilton and then fled to avoid arrest.

Answer these questions to check your understanding of the entire section.

1. **Theorizing** Why do you think Sacagawea was chosen as a guide for Lewis and Clark?

   _____

   _____

   _____

2. **Determining Cause and Effect** Why was Napoleon willing to sell the entire Louisiana Territory to the United States?

   _____

   _____

   _____

Persuasive Writing

Assume that you are a Federalist living in Massachusetts. Decide whether you are for or against seceding from the Union. In the space provided, write a letter to other Federalists to convince them to support your position.

_____

_____

_____

_____

_____

_____

_____

_____

_____

_____

_____

A Time of Conflict

Essential Question

What were the challenges to the nation's stability during the late 1700s and early 1800s?

Directions: As you read, complete a graphic organizer like the one below to illustrate the challenges facing the United States during the late 1700s and early 1800s.

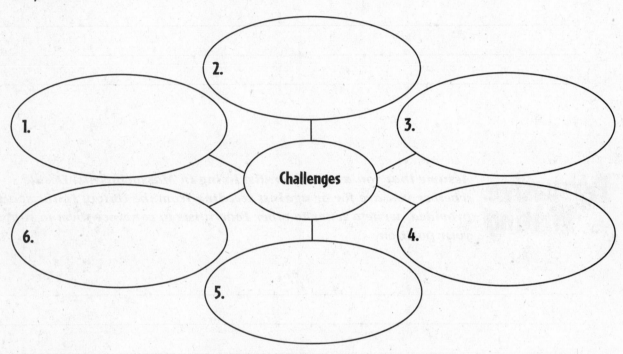

1.
2.
3.
4.
5.
6.
Challenges

 **Notes**

Read to Learn

Americans on Foreign Seas *(pages 287–288)*

Determining Cause and Effect

In the third paragraph, find a cause and an effect. Underline the cause you identified and double underline its effect.

Pirates and dangerous storms threatened ships in the early 1800s. Even so, Americans continued to travel by sea because they depended on trade with other countries. Tea, silk, furs and other goods sold well and earned high profits.

War between France and Britain in the 1790s helped American trade. Many French and British merchant ships were kept at home to avoid enemy attacks. Americans took advantage of the situation and increased their trade.

Pirates from Tripoli and the other Barbary Coast states of North Africa demanded **tribute,** or protection money, to allow ships to pass safely through the Mediterranean Sea. The United

 **Notes** | # Read to Learn

Americans on Foreign Seas (continued)

States and European nations agreed to pay the tribute. They felt it was cheaper to pay than to go to war. In 1801 Tripoli asked the United States to pay more tribute. Jefferson refused. Tripoli then declared war on the United States.

In 1804 pirates captured the *Philadelphia,* a U.S. warship. They took the ship to Tripoli and threw the crew in jail. Stephen Decatur, a U.S. Navy captain, led a group that burned the ship to stop pirates from using it. In 1805 the war ended. Tripoli agreed to stop asking for tribute, but they forced the United States to pay $60,000 for the return of the prisoners.

Freedom of the Seas (pages 288–290)

Contrasting

How was the Embargo Act different from the Nonintercourse Act?

_____

_____

Britain and France went to war in 1803. The United States did not side with either country. America was able to continue trade because of **neutral rights.** These are rights that allow a nation not involved in a conflict to continue to sail the seas. By 1805, Britain and France grew tired of America's neutrality. Both countries began searching U.S. ships that traded with the other country.

Many sailors deserted from Britain's navy. The British began to search U.S. ships for deserters and then forced the men to return to the British navy. This practice of forcing people to serve in the navy was called **impressment.** While searching American ships, the British also impressed thousands of U.S. citizens.

In 1807 the captain of an American ship, the *Chesapeake,* refused to let the British search his ship. The British fired, killing three crew members. Secretary of State James Madison and other Americans were furious. Many Americans demanded war against Britain. Instead, Jefferson tried to hurt Britain by banning the trade of all agricultural products. The Embargo Act was passed in 1807. An **embargo** forbids trade with another country. The Embargo Act banned imports from and exports to all foreign countries. The embargo was a disaster. It wiped out American trade with other countries, while Britain simply turned to Latin America for agricultural goods. Congress then approved the Nonintercourse Act. This act only banned trade with Britain, France, and their colonies. But it was unsuccessful too.

Jefferson decided not to run for a third term. In 1809 James Madison became president.

Copyright © Glencoe/McGraw-Hill, a division of The McGraw-Hill Companies, Inc.

Chapter 9, Section 3

95

Notes

Read to Learn

War Fever *(pages 291–293)*

Identifying

What challenges did James Madison face as he came into office?

_____

_____

_____

Madison faced many troubles when he became president. America was near the point of war with Britain and France. Problems also existed in the West. Chief Tecumseh built an alliance of Native Americans to stop white settlers from moving into Native American lands. William Henry Harrison, the governor of the Indiana Territory, attacked Prophetstown, a village founded by Tecumseh's brother. The Americans won this fight, called the Battle of Tippecanoe. But it caused Tecumseh to join forces with the British.

Federalists opposed conflict with Britain, but Henry Clay and John Calhoun were among the Republicans who called for war. This group, known as the War Hawks, wanted to expand the nation's power. Their **nationalism,** or loyalty to their country, appealed to American patriotism. In 1812 President Madison asked for a declaration of war. The British had decided to stop searching U.S. ships, but the news did not reach America quickly enough. War was declared.

Section Wrap-Up

Answer these questions to check your understanding of the entire section.

1. **Differentiating** Explain how the war between Britain and France affected American trade in the 1790s. How did that change in the early 1800s?

_____

_____

2. **Drawing Conclusions** What was the outcome of the Embargo Act? Do you think Jefferson was happy with its results? Why or why not?

_____

_____

Informative Writing

On a separate sheet of paper, write a story about events in the Indiana Territory from the perspective of Native Americans. Describe how the Native Americans might have felt as white settlers moved into the land and what they felt they had to do to protect the land.

The War of 1812

Essential Question

How did the United States benefit from its victory in the War of 1812?

Directions: As you read, fill in a graphic organizer like the one below to show three ways the United States benefited from its victory in the War of 1812.

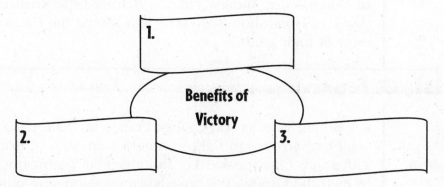

1.

Benefits of Victory

2.

3.

Notes

Read to Learn

War Begins (pages 295–296)

Identifying

Which of the following had a negative impact on American troops at the beginning of the war?

❏ *lack of weapons*
❏ *aging leaders*
❏ *underestimation of British*
❏ *widespread illness*
❏ *poorly trained troops*
❏ *short supply of soldiers*
❏ *limited support from president*

The War Hawks felt that they could quickly defeat Britain. But Americans were unprepared for war. The regular army had less than 7,000 troops, and the states had between 50,000 and 100,000 poorly trained militia. Commanders who had served during the American Revolution were too old to fight. Americans also underestimated the strength of the British and Native Americans.

The war began in July 1812. Two attempts to invade Canada were unsuccessful. Leaders decided that they needed to take control of Lake Erie to advance into Canada. Oliver Hazard Perry was in charge of the Lake Erie naval forces. He was ordered to take the lake from the British. His ships defeated the British naval force in September 1813. The British and Native American forces tried to pull back from the Detroit area, but General Harrison stopped them. In this battle, known as the Battle of Thames, Tecumseh was killed.

Another victory for the Americans took place in the town of York, what is now Toronto, Canada. There, American troops burned the parliament buildings.

Read to Learn

War Begins (continued)

The U.S. Navy had three of the fastest **frigates,** or warships. These warships and **privateers,** or armed private ships, captured or destroyed many British ships. This boosted American morale.

Before his death, Tecumseh had talked with the Creeks about forming a confederation. This plan died with Tecumseh. In March 1814, Andrew Jackson defeated the Creeks at the Battle of Horseshoe Bend. The loss forced the Creeks to give up most of their lands.

The British Offensive (pages 296–298)

Stating

Why did the British end the war?

_____

_____

Sequencing

Write a number before each battle location to list the order in which they occurred.

___ *Plattsburg*

___ *Lake Erie*

___ *New Orleans*

___ *Washington, D.C.*

___ *Horseshoe Bend*

Britain won its war against France in 1814. It was able to send more troops to fight in America. In August, British troops sailed into Chesapeake Bay and attacked Washington, D.C. They burned the Capitol, the president's mansion, and other buildings before they left the city.

The British moved on to Baltimore, but the Americans kept them from taking the city. Francis Scott Key watched the bombs burst over Fort McHenry. When he saw the U.S. flag still flying the next morning, he wrote a poem called "The Star-Spangled Banner." Congress made "The Star-Spangled Banner" the national anthem in 1931.

British troops moved to capture the city of Plattsburg on Lake Champlain. The American navy on the lake defeated the British fleet, and the British retreated. After this battle, the British decided the war was too costly and not really necessary.

In December 1814, a peace agreement called the Treaty of Ghent was signed between the United States and Britain. The treaty did not change any existing borders. It also did not mention other issues like the impressment of sailors.

Before word of the treaty reached America, one last battle was fought in New Orleans. During the Battle of New Orleans, American troops under Andrew Jackson hid behind cotton bales that protected them from bullets. The British soldiers were out in the open, and hundreds were killed. The American victory made Andrew Jackson a hero.

Federalists had opposed "Mr. Madison's War" from the beginning. In December 1814, they met at the Hartford Convention. Some wanted to secede from, or leave, the Union, but most did not. They wrote a list of changes for the Constitution. Their complaints seemed unpatriotic, especially after the victory of the war. The Federalists lost respect, and the party weakened. The War Hawks took over the Republican Party and carried on the

The British Offensive (continued)

Federalist idea of a strong national government. They favored trade, western expansion, development of the economy, and a strong military.

After the War of 1812, Americans felt a new sense of patriotism and a strong national identity. The United States also gained respect from other countries around the world.

Section Wrap-Up

Answer these questions to check your understanding of the entire section.

1. **Analyzing** Why was the death of Tecumseh significant?

   _____

   _____

2. **Determining Cause and Effect** Why did the Federalist Party weaken after the War of 1812?

   _____

   _____

Expository Writing

On a separate sheet of paper, write the words to "The Star-Spangled Banner." Analyze each line of the song and think about how it relates to what Francis Scott Key witnessed at Fort McHenry. Then in the space below, rewrite each line in your own words and explain the significance of each.

_____

_____

_____

_____

_____

_____

Chapter 10, Section 1 (Pages 304–309)
Economic Growth

Essential Question

What effects did the Industrial Revolution have on the U. S. economy?

Directions: As you read, complete a graphic organizer like the one below to explain the effects of the Industrial Revolution on the United States economy.

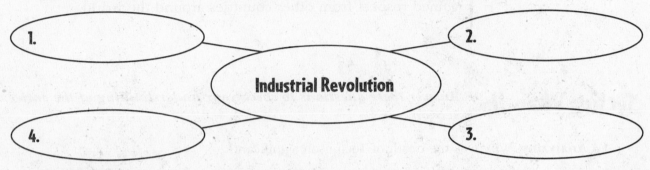

Notes

Read to Learn

The Growth of Industry (pages 305–307)

Drawing Conclusions

How did interchangeable parts alter the way goods were made?

_____

_____

_____

_____

_____

Before the mid-1700s, people made cloth and other goods in their homes or in workshops. In the mid-1700s, the way goods were made began to change. The changes began in Great Britain. The British began using machines to do some of the work in making cloth, such as spinning. They built textile mills along rivers for waterpower to run their machines. People left homes to work in the mills and earn money. This big change in how things were made is known as the Industrial Revolution.

The Industrial Revolution started in the United States around 1800. The changes began in New England. The region's poor soil made farming hard. People looked for other kinds of work. New England had rivers and streams for waterpower to run machinery in new factories. It was close to resources, such as coal and iron. The area also had many ports that could ship goods.

The invention of new machines led to the Industrial Revolution. In 1793 Eli Whitney invented the **cotton gin.** This machine removed seeds from cotton fiber. Whitney also invented **interchangeable parts.** These were identical machine parts that could be put together quickly to make a complete product. This made it easier to produce many goods on a large scale. It also lowered the price of the goods.

The Growth of Industry (continued)

Listing

What are the main parts of a free enterprise system?

1. _____

2. _____

3. _____

4. _____

In 1790 Congress passed a patent law to protect the rights of inventors. A **patent** gives an inventor the sole legal right to the invention and its profits for a certain period of time. Samuel Slater, a worker in Britain, memorized the design of machines used in the factory where he worked. He brought this knowledge to a cotton mill in the United States. There, he copied the British machines that made cotton thread. Francis Cabot Lowell made Slater's idea even better. All the steps of cloth making were done under one roof in Lowell's textile plant. A system in which all manufacturing steps are brought together in one place is called a **factory system.**

Industrial growth needs an economic system that allows competition with little government interference. **Capitalism** is the economic system of the United States. Under this system, people put their **capital,** or money, into a business in the hope that it will make a profit. **Free enterprise** is another term used to describe the American economy. The main elements of free enterprise are competition, profit, private property, and economic freedom.

Agriculture Expands (pages 307–308)

Identifying

What invention increased cotton production in the South?

_____

_____

Many people went to work in factories in the 1800s, but agriculture was still the main economic activity in the United States. Farms tended to be small in the Northeast. Textile industries grew in New England and Europe. This growth led to increased cotton production in the South. The cotton gin made it faster and easier to clean cotton fiber. Farming also expanded in the West. Southerners who wanted new land moved west to grow cotton. Some farmers in the West also raised cash crops such as corn and wheat.

Economic Independence *(pages 308–309)*

Explaining

What were some of the good and bad things about cities in the early 1800s?

_____

_____

_____

_____

_____

Small investors began to finance new businesses. They invested their money in the hope of making profits. Large businesses called corporations began to develop. The corporations made it easier to sell **stock,** or shares of ownership in a company.

The growth of factories and trade led to the growth of cities. Many cities developed near rivers because factories could use waterpower to get their goods to markets more easily. Older cities, such as New York, grew as centers of commerce and trade. In the West, towns, such as Cincinnati, benefited from their location on major rivers. These towns grew rapidly as farmers shipped their products by water.

Cities at that time had no sewers to carry away waste. Diseases like cholera sometimes killed many people. Many buildings were made of wood, and few cities had fire departments. Fires spread quickly. The good things cities had to offer generally outweighed the bad things. Cities had a variety of jobs to choose from. They also had places, like museums and shops, where people could enjoy themselves.

Section Wrap-Up *Answer these questions to check your understanding of the entire section.*

1. **Determining Cause and Effect** Why did the Industrial Revolution begin in New England?

   _____

   _____

2. **Analyzing** How did factories and trade lead to the growth of cities?

   _____

   _____

Descriptive Writing

It is the early 1800s, and you live in New England. On a separate sheet of paper, write a letter to a friend in which you describe the changes you see as a result of the Industrial Revolution.

Westward Bound

Essential Question

How did land and water transportation affect westward expansion?

Directions: As you read, complete the time line below to identify three major developments in transportation that affected westward expansion during the 1800s.

1800   1810   1820   1830
  |———————|———————|———————|———————|
        1807   1818   1825

Notes

Read to Learn

Moving West (pages 313–315)

Finding the Main Idea

Write the main idea of the passage.

_____

_____

_____

_____

Nearly 4 million people lived in the United States in 1790, according to the first **census.** A census is the official count of a population. Most Americans at that time lived east of the Appalachian Mountains. That pattern soon changed. More settlers headed west. By 1820, the population of the United States had more than doubled to about 10 million people. Almost 2 million of these people lived west of the Appalachians.

Traveling west was not easy. The United States needed decent roads to move people and goods inland. Some companies built **turnpikes,** or toll roads. The fees travelers paid to use the roads were spent to build other roads. In 1803 Ohio asked the federal government to build a national road to connect it to the East. Construction on the National Road started in 1811, and the first section opened in 1818.

Traveling by wagon and horse on roads was long and not very comfortable. Traveling on the rivers was far better. It was also easier to carry large loads of farm goods on boats and barges than in wagons. However, river travel had two problems. First, most large rivers in the United States flowed north to south, but most people and goods headed east to west. Second, traveling upstream against the river current was hard and slow.

Notes | Read to Learn

Moving West (continued)

Calculating

How many times faster did the Clermont *make the Hudson River trip than a sailboat would have?*

_____

_____

Robert Fulton developed the *Clermont,* a steamboat with a powerful engine. In 1807 the *Clermont* traveled up the Hudson River from New York to the city of Albany in record time. It took only 32 hours to make the trip. Using only sails, the trip would have taken four days.

The use of steamboats changed river travel. Steamboats made transportation much easier and more comfortable. Shipping goods by steamboat became cheaper and faster. Steamboats also helped river cities, like St. Louis and Cincinnati, grow.

Canals (pages 315–316)

Analyzing

How did canals improve water transportation?

_____

_____

_____

_____

Steamboats improved river transportation, but they depended on existing rivers, which flowed north to south. Steamboats could not link the eastern and western parts of the country. De Witt Clinton and other officials made a plan to link New York City with the Great Lakes area. They would build a **canal** across the state of New York. A canal is an artificial waterway.

Thousands of workers worked on building the Erie Canal. They built a series of **locks** along the canal. Locks are separate compartments used to raise or lower water levels. Boats could be raised or lowered at places where canal levels changed. The Erie Canal finally opened in 1825. Clinton used the canal to make his trip from Buffalo, New York, to Albany, New York, and then down the Hudson River to New York City.

In the 1840s, canals were reinforced to allow steamboats to travel on them. Many other canals were built. By 1850, the United States had more than 3,600 miles (5,794 km) of canals. Canals lowered the cost of shipping goods and helped spur growth in the towns along their routes.

 **Notes** | **Read to Learn**

Western Settlement (page 317)

Explaining

Why did most pioneer families settle along big rivers?

_____

_____

_____

_____

By 1820, more than 2 million people lived west of the Appalachian Mountains. Five new western states were created. Pioneers moved to the West to find a better life. Most pioneer families settled along the big rivers so they could more easily ship their crops and goods to markets. Canals allowed people to live farther away from the rivers. People usually settled with others from their home communities. Western families often gathered for social events, such as sports and sewing parties.

Section Wrap-Up

Answer these questions to check your understanding of the entire section.

1. **Determining Cause and Effect** Ohio's population increased by nearly 14 times its original number between 1800 and 1820. How and why did so many people settle in Ohio?

   _____

   _____

2. **Evaluating** What form of transportation do you think had the greatest impact on Americans in the early 1800s? Why do you think so?

   _____

   _____

 **Informative Writing**

On a separate sheet of paper, write an article explaining how transportation in the United States improved in the early 1800s.

Unity and Sectionalism

Essential Question

How were nation-building issues resolved in the early 1800s?

Directions: As you read, complete a graphic organizer like the one below
to explain how nation-building issues were resolved in the early 1800s.

Issue	Northern View	Southern View	How Resolved
Slavery in New States	1.	2.	3.
Tariffs	4.	5.	6.

 **Notes**

Read to Learn

The Era of Good Feelings (page 321)

Finding the Main Idea

Underline the sentence that is the main idea of the paragraph.

A feeling of national unity swept the United States after the War of 1812. James Monroe faced almost no opposition in the election of 1816. Support grew for tariffs to protect industries and a national bank. A Boston newspaper called these years the Era of Good Feelings. President James Monroe was a symbol of these good feelings. He toured the nation early in his term. Not since George Washington had a president done this. In 1820 Monroe easily won reelection.

Sectionalism and the American System (pages 322–324)

By 1820, the Era of Good Feelings ended because of regional differences. Most Americans felt loyal to the region where they lived. They thought of themselves as Northerners or Southerners. This loyalty to a region is called **sectionalism.**

Regions disagreed over issues. One issue was slavery. Most white Southerners supported it. They believed that the Constitution gave states the right to govern themselves. They believed that the federal government and Northerners were limiting states' rights. The regions also disagreed about other issues. These included tariffs, a national bank, and programs for internal improvements such as canals and roads.

Sectionalism and the American System (continued)

How did the views of John C. Calhoun and Daniel Webster differ?

_____

_____

_____

_____

What was the Supreme Court's ruling in McCulloch v. Maryland?

_____

_____

_____

_____

John C. Calhoun, a Southern planter, once supported the programs of the national government. However, he began to change his views in the 1820s. He began to support **state sovereignty.** This is the idea that states have the right to govern themselves. He also opposed high tariffs. Calhoun believed tariffs raised the prices of manufactured goods that Southerners could not make for themselves.

Daniel Webster, a senator from Massachusetts, supported the Tariff of 1816. He believed the tariff protected American industries from foreign competition. Webster was a great public speaker. He spoke in defense of the nation as a whole against sectional interests.

Henry Clay of Kentucky was a leader in the House of Representatives. He tried to resolve sectional conflicts. In 1820 he came up with a plan to solve the dispute over slavery. The Missouri Compromise called for Missouri to be admitted as a slave state and Maine as a free state. Clay also proposed the **American System.** This program had three parts: a tariff, internal improvements, and a national bank. Many Southerners did not agree with Clay's proposal.

The Supreme Court also became involved in sectionalism. In *McCulloch* v. *Maryland,* the Court ruled that the national government's interest comes first if there is a conflict between a state government and the national government. In *Gibbons* v. *Ogden,* the Court ruled that states could not pass laws that would interfere with the power of Congress over interstate trade. People who supported states' rights did not agree with the Court's rulings.

Foreign Affairs (page 325–326)

The United States knew it had to set up new relationships with foreign countries. The Convention of 1818 set the boundary of the Louisiana Territory between the United States and British ruled Canada at the 49th parallel. The United States and Britain agreed to keep the border without armed forces.

Spain owned East Florida and claimed West Florida. The United States argued that West Florida was part of the Louisiana Purchase. In 1810 and 1812, Americans simply added parts of West Florida to Louisiana and Mississippi. Spain took no action. General Andrew Jackson invaded Spanish East Florida. He took over two forts there. Jackson's raid showed American military strength.

Foreign Affairs (continued)

Summarizing

What was the result of the Adams-Onís Treaty?

_____

_____

_____

_____

The Adams-Onís Treaty was signed in 1819. In the treaty, the United States gained East Florida, and Spain gave up its claims to West Florida. In return, the United States gave up its claims to Spanish Texas. At the same time, Spain was losing power in Mexico. In 1821 Mexico finally gained its independence.

Simón Bolívar won independence from Spain for the present-day countries of Venezuela, Colombia, Panama, Bolivia, and Ecuador. José de San Martín won freedom from Spain for Chile and Peru. By 1824, Spain had lost control of most of South America.

In 1822 several European countries talked about a plan to help Spain take back its American colonies. President Monroe did not want more European involvement in North America. In 1823 he issued the **Monroe Doctrine.** It said that European powers could no longer set up colonies in North America and South America. It became an important part of American foreign policy.

Section Wrap-Up

Answer these questions to check your understanding of the entire section.

1. **Synthesizing** What issues caused sectional conflicts in the United States?

   _____

   _____

2. **Analyzing** Why did President Monroe issue the Monroe Doctrine?

   _____

   _____

Expository Writing

On a separate sheet of paper, write a short essay that compares the views of John C. Calhoun, Daniel Webster, and Henry Clay regarding states' rights over national interests.

Jacksonian Democracy

Essential Question

How did political beliefs and events shape Andrew Jackson's presidency?

Directions: As you read, complete a graphic organizer like the one below to show three major events of Jackson's presidency.

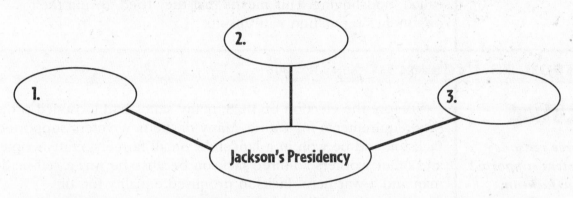

 **Notes** | **Read to Learn**

Elections of 1824 and 1828 (pages 337–339)

Summarizing

Write two to three sentences summarizing what happened in the election of 1824:

_____

_____

_____

_____

_____

In 1824 the Republican Party was the only party in the nation. Four Republicans ran for the presidency. The Republican Party nominated William H. Crawford. The other candidates were Andrew Jackson, Henry Clay, and John Quincy Adams. Different regions of the country supported these three candidates.

Jackson won the most popular votes. He also won a **plurality,** or the largest single share, of the electoral votes. However, no candidate received a **majority,** or more than half, of the electoral votes. In a case like this, the Twelfth Amendment states that the House of Representatives will choose the president. Clay and Adams struck a deal. Clay used his position as Speaker of the House to help defeat Jackson and elect Adams. Adams then appointed Clay as secretary of state. Jackson's followers believed the election was stolen and called it a "corrupt bargain."

As president, Adams proposed an ambitious program. He wanted to improve roads and waterways, create a national university, and support the sciences. His opponents thought the government should not spend money on such projects. In the end, Congress only approved money to improve roads and waterways.

 **Notes** | # Read to Learn

Elections of 1824 and 1828 (continued)

By 1828 the Republican Party had split into two parties, the Democratic-Republicans and the National Republicans. Democratic-Republicans supported Jackson and favored states' rights. National Republicans supported Adams and wanted a strong national government. Both parties used a new tactic called mudslinging. This means that they tried to ruin their opponent's reputation with insults.

Jackson as President (pages 339–340)

Listing

List three reasons new voters supported Andrew Jackson.

1. _____

_____

2. _____

_____

3. _____

_____

Before the election of 1828, many states had loosened property requirements for voting. Many of the new voters supported Jackson, and he won in a landslide. Small farmers, craftspeople, and other workers admired Jackson because he was a self-made man and a war hero. Jackson promised equality for all Americans, but only white men could vote.

Once he was president, Jackson fired many government workers and hired his supporters. This practice is called the **spoils system.** Jackson's supporters changed the way candidates were chosen. They replaced **caucuses** with **nominating conventions.** Under the caucus system, major candidates were chosen by Congress. At nominating conventions, delegates from the states choose the party's presidential candidate. This change allowed more people to help choose the candidates.

The Tariff Debate (page 341)

Contrasting

Contrast how Northeasterners and Southerners viewed the high tariff on European goods.

_____

_____

_____

A **tariff** is a fee that is paid on imported goods. Northeastern factory owners supported a high tariff on goods that were imported from Europe. The tariff made those goods more expensive than American-made goods. Southerners did not like the tariff, because it meant higher prices.

John C. Calhoun of South Carolina argued that states could **nullify,** or cancel, any federal law that was against the state's interests. In 1832 South Carolina passed the Nullification Act. It said that South Carolina would not pay the "illegal" tariffs. The state threatened to **secede,** or break away, from the Union if the federal government interfered. To avoid a crisis, Jackson backed a bill that would lower the tariff. At the same time, he had Congress pass the Force Bill. This would allow him to use the military to enforce federal laws. South Carolina accepted the new tariff but nullified the Force Bill.

Section Wrap-Up

Answer these questions to check your understanding of the entire section.

1. **Determining Cause and Effect** Why did Jackson win the presidential election of 1828 in a landslide?

   _____

   _____

   _____

2. **Analyzing** How did Jackson prevent South Carolina from seceding over tariffs, while still upholding the rights of the federal government?

   _____

   _____

   _____

In the space below, write a letter to the editor of a newspaper giving reasons why you support the election of Andrew Jackson in 1828. Assume that you are a male factory worker who can vote for the first time in this election.

_____

_____

_____

_____

_____

_____

_____

_____

_____

_____

_____

_____

Chapter 11, Section 2 (Pages 342–347)

Conflicts Over Land

Essential Question

How did Andrew Jackson's presidency affect Native Americans?

Directions: As you read, complete a graphic organizer like the one below
to show how Jackson's presidency affected different Native American groups.

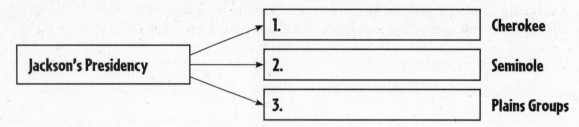

Jackson's Presidency	1. _____ **Cherokee**
	2. _____ **Seminole**
	3. _____ **Plains Groups**

Notes	**Read to Learn**

Moving Native Americans (pages 343–346)

Identifying

*Who were the Five
Civilized Tribes?*

1. _____

2. _____

3. _____

4. _____

5. _____

Identifying Central Issues

*Over what issue did
the Supreme Court
and President
Jackson disagree?*

_____

_____

_____

In the 1830s, many Native Americans still lived in the eastern United States. The "Five Civilized Tribes"—the Cherokee, Creek, Seminole, Chickasaw, and Choctaw—lived in several Southeastern states. Many white settlers wanted the Native Americans' land because it seemed more suitable for farming. They wanted the government to **relocate,** or move, Native Americans living in the Southeast to land west of the Mississippi River.

President Jackson supported this idea and pushed the Indian Removal Act through Congress. This act allowed the government to pay Native Americans to move west. Native American leaders felt forced into signing treaties that sold their land. In 1834 Congress created the Indian Territory. This was an area in Oklahoma where Native Americans were to be relocated.

The federal government had already recognized the Cherokee in Georgia as a separate nation. Georgia tried to remove the Cherokee, but the Cherokee refused to give up their land. They took their case to the Supreme Court. The Supreme Court ruled that Georgia could not interfere with the Cherokee. However, President Jackson announced that he would ignore the Supreme Court decision.

In 1835 the federal government convinced a small group of Cherokee to sign a treaty giving up their land. Most Cherokee refused to honor the treaty. In 1838 federal troops under General Winfield Scott threatened to use force if the Cherokee

Moving Native Americans *(continued)*

did not leave. The Cherokee gave in and began the march to the West. Thousands of Cherokee died during the long journey. The journey became known as the Trail of Tears.

Native American Resistance *(pages 346–347)*

Finding the Main Idea

Highlight the sentence that best expresses the main idea of this section.

Theorizing

Why do you think the Seminole people were successful in resisting removal, but other groups were not?

_____

_____

_____

_____

Some groups of Native Americans tried to resist being moved, but most were unsuccessful. In 1832 a Sauk chieftain, Black Hawk, led a group of Sauk and Fox people back to Illinois. The Illinois state militia and federal troops chased them to the Mississippi River and killed most of them as they tried to flee.

The Seminole people of Florida were the only group that successfully resisted removal. The Seminole chief, Osceola, and some of his people refused to leave Florida. The Seminole decided to go to war against the United States instead. In 1835 the Seminole joined with a group of African Americans who had run away to escape slavery. They attacked white settlements in Florida, using **guerrilla tactics.** They made surprise attacks and then retreated back into the swamps and forests. By 1842, more than 1,500 Americans had died in the Seminole wars. The government gave up and allowed some of the Seminole to remain in Florida.

By 1842, most Native Americans had been moved west. They had given up more than 100 million acres (40.47 ha) of Eastern land. In return, they had received about $68 million and 32 million acres (12.9 ha) of land west of the Mississippi. They lived on reservations there. Eventually, white settlements would expand into this land as well.

The Five Civilized Tribes were relocated to land that was already occupied by several Plains groups. Those groups agreed to let the Five Civilized Tribes live there in peace. The Five Civilized Tribes developed new governments and a police force. They also built farms and schools on their new land.

Answer these questions to check your understanding of the entire section.

1. **Explaining** What was the Indian Removal Act, and how was it used?

   _____

   _____

   _____

2. **Evaluating** Do you think Native Americans were adequately paid for giving up their land? Why or why not?

   _____

   _____

   _____

In the space below, describe the events leading up to the removal of the Cherokee from their land.

_____

_____

_____

_____

_____

_____

_____

_____

_____

_____

_____

_____

Chapter 11, Section 3 (Pages 348–352)

Jackson and the Bank

Essential Question

How do economic issues affect the president and presidential elections?

Directions: As you read, complete a graphic organizer like the one below to explain how economic issues affected the presidential elections of 1836 and 1840.

Economic Issues		Effect on Presidential Election
1.	→	**2.** 1836
3.	→	**4.** 1840

Notes   **Read to Learn**

War Against the Bank (pages 349–351)

Summarizing

Write three to four sentences summarizing the plan of Clay and Webster and its results.

_____
_____
_____
_____
_____
_____
_____
_____

President Jackson attacked the Bank of the United States for many reasons. The Bank was powerful. It held the federal government's money and controlled much of the nation's money supply. It had strict lending policies. It was run by private bankers, not by elected officials. Jackson believed the Bank was an organization of wealthy Easterners. He especially disliked the wealthy Bank president, Nicholas Biddle.

Senators Henry Clay and Daniel Webster believed they could use the Bank to defeat Jackson in the 1832 presidential election. They persuaded Biddle to apply for a new charter for the Bank in 1832, four years earlier than needed. The senators believed the Bank was supported by the people. They thought that Jackson's **veto** of the charter would lead to his defeat in the election.

The plan backfired. Most people supported Jackson's veto of the Bank's charter, and he was reelected. The Bank closed in 1836.

Jackson decided not to run for reelection in 1836. The Democrats chose Martin Van Buren as their candidate. He faced three different candidates from the new Whig Party. Van Buren won easily.

War Against the Bank (continued)

Distinguishing Fact From Opinion

Circle the factual statement below. Underline the opinion.

The government should not interfere with the nation's economy.

During a depression, business and employment fall to a very low level.

The following year, the Panic of 1837 led to an economic **depression.** A depression is a period in which business and employment fall to a very low level. Land values dropped, businesses closed, banks failed, and many people lost their jobs.

Van Buren believed in **laissez-faire,** the principle that the government should interfere as little as possible in the nation's economy. During the crisis, he persuaded Congress to start an independent federal treasury. The government would store its money in the federal treasury instead of private banks. Private banks would not be able to use government funds to back their banknotes. He believed this would help prevent bank failures in the future. However, the plan was criticized by many Democrats as well as Whigs. This opened the door for Whigs to win the presidency in 1840.

The Whigs Take Power (pages 351-352)

Identifying

Circle the political party of each of the men listed below:

Martin Van Buren
Democrat   Whig

William Henry Harrison
Democrat   Whig

John Tyler
Democrat   Whig

Henry Clay
Democrat   Whig

James Polk
Democrat   Whig

William Henry Harrison was the Whig candidate for president in 1840. He was a hero of the War of 1812 and had helped win the Battle of Tippecanoe. John Tyler was his running mate. The Whigs' campaign slogan was "Tippecanoe and Tyler, Too." The Whigs needed to gain the support of many of the farmers and laborers who had voted for Jackson. The Whigs adopted the log cabin as their symbol to show that their candidate was a "man of the people." The log cabin campaign worked, and Harrison defeated Van Buren in the election.

Harrison delivered his inauguration speech on a bitterly cold day without a hat or coat. He died of pneumonia 32 days later. John Tyler became the first vice president to become president because the elected president died in office. Tyler had once been a Democrat. As president, he vetoed several bills sponsored by Whigs in Congress. Whig Party leaders were furious and expelled him from the Party.

Whigs in Congress could not agree on their goals. They often voted based on where they came from, not as a party. This division may explain why the next Whig presidential candidate, Henry Clay, lost the 1844 election to Democrat James Polk.

Section Wrap-Up

Answer these questions to check your understanding of the entire section.

1. **Explaining** Why did Jackson oppose the Bank of the United States?

   _____

   _____

   _____

2. **Speculating** Do you think the Whigs would have lost power in 1844 if Harrison had lived? Why or why not?

   _____

   _____

   _____

In the space below, compare and contrast the reasons why the Democratic Party lost power in 1840 to the reasons why the Whig Party lost power in 1844.

_____

_____

_____

_____

_____

_____

_____

_____

_____

_____

_____

_____

_____

The Oregon Country

Essential Question

How did the belief in Manifest Destiny influence western settlement?

Directions: As you read, complete a graphic organizer like the one below to identify the countries with claims on the Oregon Country.

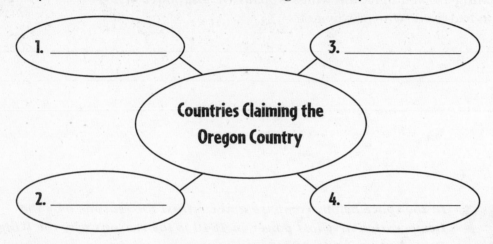

1. _____

2. _____

3. _____

4. _____

Countries Claiming the Oregon Country

Notes

Read to Learn

Rivalry in the Northwest *(pages 359–361)*

Differentiating

Complete the following sentences.

1. The countries that gave up all claims to Oregon were

_____ *and*

_____.

2. The countries that agreed to joint occupation of the Oregon Country were

_____ *and*

_____.

The Oregon Country was the huge area between the Pacific Ocean and the Rocky Mountains. It included the area north of present-day California and into British Columbia. In the early 1800s, four nations laid claim to the Oregon Country: the United States, Great Britain, Spain, and Russia.

Many Americans wanted to control the Oregon Country. The United States reached a deal with Spain for the land. In the Adams-Onís Treaty of 1819, Spain agreed to set the limits of its territory at what is now California's northern border. Spain also gave up all claims to Oregon. Then, in 1824, Russia also gave up its claim to the land south of Alaska.

The United States worked out an agreement with Great Britain in 1818. In this plan, both countries agreed to **joint occupation.** This meant that people from both countries could settle there. Americans began pouring into the Oregon Country.

The first people to reach the Oregon Country were fur traders. British and American merchants set up trading posts for the fur trade. American adventurers joined the trade. These people spent most of their time in the Rocky Mountains trapping

Rivalry in the Northwest (continued)

Making Inferences

Why were mountain men often picked to be guides through the Oregon Country?

_____

_____

beaver for furs. Called **mountain men,** these people worked hard. They gathered once a year for a **rendezvous** (RAHN•dih•voo), or meeting. Here they carried out business and shared news with old friends.

Over time, most of the beaver were killed, and mountain men could no longer make a living from trapping. Some men moved to Oregon and settled on farms. Others found work as guides. They led new settlers who were moving west. These men created passages west across the land. The most popular route was the Oregon Trail. Other routes were the Santa Fe Trail and the California Trail.

Oregon and Manifest Destiny (pages 361–363)

Analyzing

Explain what the term "Oregon fever" meant.

_____

_____

_____

_____

Some of the first settlers in the Oregon Country were missionaries. These Christians wanted to spread their religion to the Native Americans. New settlers unknowingly brought measles to the area. The disease killed many children of the Cayuse tribe. The Cayuse attacked the missionaries in 1847. Despite this attack, the flood of settlers still moved west.

In the early 1840s, "Oregon fever" swept across the Mississippi Valley. Tens of thousands of people, called **emigrants,** decided to move from the United States to Oregon. They loaded up their **prairie schooners,** or canvas-covered wagons, and made the long, hard trip across the Oregon Trail.

About this time, Americans' ideas about the mission of the nation changed. In colonial times, Americans thought the nation should serve as a model for freedom. In the 1840s, this idea changed. Many Americans now believed that the nation should spread freedom. They wanted the country to spread over and possess the whole of the continent. This idea was called **Manifest Destiny.**

Many Americans wanted the United States to own all of Oregon. In 1844 Democratic presidential candidate James K. Polk supported this idea. Henry Clay, Polk's Whig opponent, did not take a stand on the Oregon issue. Clay lost much Whig support, and Polk won the election. Polk focused on making Oregon part of the United States. In 1846 a border was set between the American and British parts of Oregon.

Answer these questions to check your understanding of the entire section.

1. **Making Inferences** Why did the Cayuse attack the missionaries in Oregon?

   _____

   _____

   _____

2. **Contrasting** How did colonial Americans' idea of the nation's mission differ from that of pioneers of the 1840s?

   _____

   _____

   _____

Take the role of a mountain man. In the space below, write a postcard to your family in the United States and describe the latest events in your life as a beaver trapper.

_____

_____

_____

_____

_____

_____

_____

_____

_____

_____

_____

_____

_____

_____

Independence for Texas

Essential Question

Why did Texans fight for their independence from Mexico?

Directions: As you read, complete a graphic organizer like the one below to identify the four conditions placed on settlers in Texas under Mexican law.

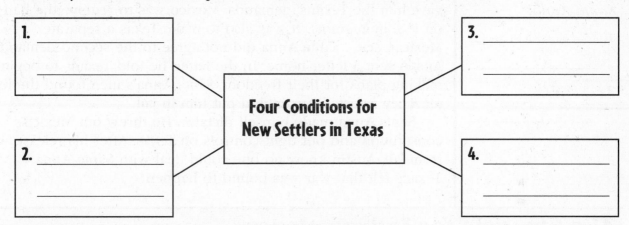

1. _____

2. _____

3. _____

4. _____

Four Conditions for New Settlers in Texas

 **Notes**

Read to Learn

A Clash of Cultures (pages 367–368)

Sequencing

Write the year that each event occurred in the blank provided.

1. _____ *Mexico wins its independence from Spain.*

2. _____ *Mexico issues a decree to stop U.S. immigration.*

3. _____ *General Santa Anna becomes president of Mexico.*

Few people lived in Texas in the early 1800s. Most residents were **Tejanos** (teh•HAH•nohs), or Mexicans. Some were Native Americans. Others were **empresarios,** or people to whom the Spanish government had given Texas land grants.

Moses Austin, an American, got the first land grant in 1821. This was the same year that Mexico won its freedom from Spain. Moses died before he could set up his colony. Moses's son, Stephen F. Austin, then got approval from the new Mexican government to settle in Texas. Austin brought in 300 American families and set up a colony there.

Mexico began selling land to settlers at very low prices. All the settlers had to do was agree to some conditions. They would have to learn Spanish and become Mexican citizens. They would have to convert to Catholicism, the Mexican religion. Settlers would also have to obey Mexican law.

By 1830, most people who lived in Texas were Americans. The Americans had not met the conditions that Mexico set up. This alarmed Mexican officials. They issued a **decree,** or official order, to stop immigration from the United States. At the same

A Clash of Cultures (continued)

Listing

In the spaces below, list the two demands that Texans made of Santa Anna.

1. _____

   _____

2. _____

   _____

time, the decree offered Mexicans and Europeans land grants. Mexico also taxed U.S. goods. These policies made the Texans angry.

General Antonio López de Santa Anna became president of Mexico in 1833. At a meeting with Santa Anna, Stephen F. Austin gave him the Texans' demands. Mexico was to remove the ban on U.S. immigrants. It was also to make Texas a separate Mexican state. Santa Anna did not agree to the second demand. Austin sent a letter home. In the letter, he told Texans to begin making plans for their freedom. Santa Anna's men found the letter. They arrested Austin and put him in jail.

Santa Anna made himself dictator. He threw out Mexico's constitution and put tight controls on Texas. After his release from jail, Austin knew no one could deal with Santa Anna. Texans felt that war was bound to happen.

The Struggle for Independence (pages 369–371)

Interpreting

Why do you think the Texans shouted "Remember the Alamo!" when they attacked Santa Anna's troops?

_____

_____

_____

_____

During 1835, unrest among Texans often turned into open conflict. Santa Anna sent in troops to punish the rebels.

In December 1835, the Texans freed San Antonio from Mexican forces. Santa Anna responded. He marched to San Antonio with a large army and reached the city in February. There, he found a Texas force of about 180 men in a mission called the Alamo. The Texas military was small and had only rifles as weapons, but they fought for 12 days. On March 6, 1836, Mexican soldiers stormed the fort. Only a few women and children and some servants were left alive.

During the battle at the Alamo, Texas leaders were meeting to write a constitution. Four days before the Alamo fell, they declared freedom from Mexico. The Republic of Texas began.

The Texans named Sam Houston as commander of Texas forces. Houston ordered troops at Goliad to leave their position. In retreat, they met Santa Anna's army. After a fierce fight, several hundred Texans surrendered. Santa Anna had these men killed. This action, called the Goliad Massacre, made the Texans very angry.

Houston gathered troops in San Jacinto (SAN huh•SIHN•to). On April 21, 1836, the Texans made a surprise attack on Santa Anna's men. As they advanced, the Texans shouted, "Remember the Alamo!" The Texans defeated the Mexican troops. Santa Anna signed a treaty on May 14, 1836.

The Struggle for Independence (continued)

In September 1836, Texans elected Sam Houston as their president. Houston asked the United States to **annex,** or take control of, Texas. President Andrew Jackson refused this request. He knew that adding Texas, a slave state, would upset the balance of power in Congress. The debate continued over Texas statehood until 1844. James K. Polk, the presidential candidate, was for Manifest Destiny. He also wanted to add Texas to the Union. Texas became a state in 1845.

Section Wrap-Up

Answer these questions to check your understanding of the entire section.

1. **Analyzing** Why did the Mexican government want to stop U.S. immigration to Texas?

   _____

   _____

2. **Assessing** During the siege of the Alamo, Commander Travis sent messages that asked for aid from Texans and the United States. Why do you believe that aid was not given?

   _____

   _____

   _____

   _____

   _____

Persuasive Writing *On a separate sheet of paper, write a flyer you will post to convince Texans that independence from Mexico is needed. Use facts and graphics to support your case.*

Chapter 12, Section 3 (Pages 372–377)

War With Mexico

Essential Question

How did Mexican lands in the West become part of the United States?

Directions: As you read, complete a graphic organizer like the one below to describe President Polk's three-part war plan with Mexico.

Polk's War Plan	1. _____
	2. _____
	3. _____

 **Notes** **Read to Learn**

The New Mexico Territory (page 373)

Naming

Underline in the text the name of the first American trader to reach Santa Fe.

In the 1800s, New Mexico was the large area between the Texas and California territories. Spanish conquistadors had made the region a Spanish colony in the 1500s. They founded a settlement there called Santa Fe. Once free from Spain, Mexico won the New Mexico territory. Mexico welcomed Americans into the area. It hoped that trade would boost the economy.

William Becknell was the first American trader to reach Santa Fe in 1821. His route to the settlement was known as the Santa Fe Trail. Beginning in Missouri, the trail crossed the Rocky Mountains. As more traders came to Santa Fe, the trail became a busy route. Americans also began settling in the area. They hoped it would one day be part of the United States.

California's Spanish Culture (page 374)

Listing

List two things Frémont found inviting about California.

1. _____

2. _____

California became a state in the new Mexican nation. Mexican settlers in California set up huge estates called **ranchos.** The **rancheros,** or ranch owners, treated the Native Americans who worked for them almost like enslaved people.

In the 1840s, more Americans came to California. Army officer John C. Frémont wrote of the area's mild climate and vast resources. Americans talked about annexing California. They wanted the United States to stretch from the Atlantic to the Pacific.

124

Chapter 12, Section 3

Copyright © Glencoe/McGraw-Hill, a division of The McGraw-Hill Companies, Inc.

Notes | Read to Learn

War With Mexico *(pages 375–377)*

Finding the Main Idea

Circle the sentence below that best states the main idea of the second paragraph.

A. Mexico threatened to reclaim Texas.

B. U.S. relations with Mexico were tense.

C. Polk wanted war with Mexico.

D. Polk offered a deal to Mexico, but Mexico refused the offer.

U.S.–Mexico relations were tense in the early 1800s. Both countries argued over the border between Texas and Mexico. President Polk wanted California and New Mexico and plotted to get them. He decided to go to war for the land, but he wanted Mexico to make the first strike.

Polk offered Mexico a deal. The United States would pay Mexico $30 million for California and New Mexico if Mexico would agree to make the Rio Grande River the Texas border. In addition, the United States would take over Mexico's war debts to Americans. Mexico did not like the offer. It refused and threatened to reclaim Texas.

Polk sent troops into the disputed area between Texas and Mexico. On April 24, 1846, Mexican troops attacked U.S. forces. On May 11, Congress declared war on Mexico. Polk went ahead with his war plan. First, U.S. troops would secure the Texas border. Then they would take New Mexico and California. Finally, they would seize Mexico City, the capital of Mexico.

In June 1864, a group of Americans took a northern town in California and declared that California was independent. They called it the Bear Flag Republic. In July 1846, U.S. forces landed in California. They took over the republic and put down a revolt by the **Californios**, or the Mexicans who lived in California. In August 1846, U.S. forces captured Santa Fe. By the end of 1847, the U.S. army under General Winfield Scott had taken Mexico City.

Mexico surrendered. The Treaty of Guadalupe Hidalgo was signed in 1848. Mexico agreed to the Rio Grande as the border between Texas and Mexico. In what is called the Mexican Cession, Mexico also **ceded**, or gave, California and New Mexico to the United States for $15 million. Then, in 1853, Mexico sold the United States a strip of land south of New Mexico. This purchase, called the Gadsden Purchase, brought the U.S. mainland to its current size.

Section Wrap-Up

Answer these questions to check your understanding of the entire section.

1. **Analyzing** How did Manifest Destiny affect New Mexico and California territories?

   _____

   _____

2. **Making Inferences** How did the offer that President Polk made to Mexico fit into his plot to gain New Mexico and California?

   _____

   _____

   _____

Informative Writing

In the space below, write a newspaper article informing the American public about the Treaty of Guadalupe Hidalgo.

_____

_____

_____

_____

_____

_____

_____

_____

_____

_____

_____

_____

_____

_____

California and Utah

Essential Question

How did the discovery of gold affect California's history?

Directions: As you read, complete a graphic organizer like the one below to identify the land of origin of the immigrants that came to California after gold was discovered.

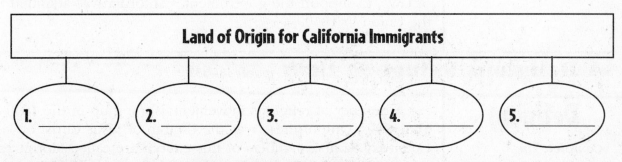

Land of Origin for California Immigrants

1. _____
2. _____
3. _____
4. _____
5. _____

 **Notes**

Read to Learn

California Gold Rush (pages 379–380)

Making Connections

What effect did the Gold Rush have on California's population?

_____

_____

_____

_____

Gold was found in California in 1848. People from all over the world poured into California. Those who arrived in 1849 were called **forty-niners.** Most were Americans. Others came from China, Australia, Europe, South America, and Mexico.

The Californios became U.S. citizens. They had rights to their lands. The Land Law of 1851 gave an exam board the right to review the land rights of Californios. A new settler sometimes claimed a Californio's land. To settle the dispute, the two parties would go to court. The Californios had to prove their land claim. Some had no proof and lost their land.

The Gold Rush also affected California's cities. Trade and populations in cities grew. New communities, called **boomtowns**, rose quickly. Boomtown merchants made huge profits. For instance, Levi Strauss got rich selling his "Levi's," or sturdy pants. Though much gold was found in California, few forty-niners became rich. They lived in hardship in mining towns. These towns had no police or prisons. As a result, citizens formed groups known as **vigilantes** (VIH•juh•LAN•teez) to protect themselves.

Notes | Read to Learn

California Gold Rush (continued)

The Gold Rush had lasting effects on California. Agriculture, shipping, and trade grew due to the demand for food and goods. Many who came looking for gold stayed in California and farmed or ran a business.

Rapid growth led to the need for a better government. California applied for statehood. It had a constitution, or a list of laws, to support the government. California was admitted to the Union in 1850.

A Religious Refuge in Utah (pages 381–382)

Defining

Complete the sentence below.

The practice of having more than one wife is called

_____.

Sequencing

Circle the event that happened first.

Mormons traveled to Utah.

Utah became a state.

Joseph Smith was killed.

A number of religious movements sprang up in the 1830s and 1840s. One of these was the Church of Jesus Christ of Latter-day Saints. Members of this church are called Mormons. As founder of the church, Joseph Smith began preaching Mormon ideas in 1830. He published the *Book of Mormon.* Smith said the book was a translation of words on golden plates he received from an angel. The text told about the coming of God and the need to build a kingdom on Earth to receive him.

Smith wanted to use his visions to build a new society. He believed that people should share their property with others. He also believed in polygamy, having more than one wife. This idea angered many people, and Mormons gave up this practice.

Smith created a Mormon community in New York. Neighbors did not approve of the religion and forced the Mormons to leave. They next settled in Illinois, but they were treated poorly there. A mob of local residents killed Smith in 1844. Brigham Young took over as head of the Mormons.

The Mormons wanted religious freedom. Young decided to move the Mormons west. He set his sights on the Great Salt Lake in Utah. About 12,000 Mormons made the trip to Utah in 1846. It was the largest single migration in American history. The Mormons made their way along a path later known as the Mormon Trail. They arrived in Utah in 1847 and made a claim on land they called Deseret.

Life in Deseret was difficult, but the Mormons worked hard and thrived. They farmed and built irrigation systems to water their crops. They planned their towns, taxed their property, and controlled the use of resources. They also sold supplies to forty-niners who passed through Utah.

The United States gained Utah from Mexico after the war in 1848. Congress established the Utah Territory in 1850. Brigham Young was made governor of Utah. Many Mormon communities

A Religious Refuge in Utah (continued)

were built in the Utah region. The Mormons often had conflicts with the federal government. In 1857 and 1858, war almost broke out between the Mormons and the U.S. Army. Not until 1896 did Utah become a state.

Section Wrap-Up

Answer these questions to check your understanding of the entire section.

1. **Analyzing Primary Sources** Howard Stansbury visited the Utah area in 1855. He wrote about the "indomitable energy . . . which seems to possess the entire Mormon community." Based on your reading about the Mormons, what do you think the word *indomitable* means?

   _____

   _____

2. **Making Connections** The Mormons continued to move west to find religious freedom. For what other reasons would people migrate?

   _____

   _____

On a separate sheet of paper, write a travel brochure to advertise a California boomtown. Be sure to include vivid descriptions of the town's features that might attract visitors.

The North's Economy

Essential Question

What innovations in industry, travel, and communications changed the lives of Americans in the 1800s?

Directions: As you read, complete a chart like the one below to name the innovations in industry, travel, and communications that changed the lives of Americans in the 1800s.

Innovations

Industry	Travel	Technology
1. _____	1. _____	1. _____
2. _____	2. _____	
3. _____	3. _____	
	4. _____	

Notes

Read to Learn

Technology and Industry (pages 389–392)

Describing

Describe the three phases of industrialization.

1. _____

_____

2. _____

_____

3. _____

_____

Many new ideas and methods in industry and technology developed during the 1800s. These ideas and methods changed the way Americans worked, traveled, and communicated.

Industrialization came about in three phases. In the first phase, tasks were divided among workers. In the second phase, factories were built to bring specialized workers together. In the third phase, some of the work was completed by machines. Workers tended the machines instead of making the products. Each phase allowed manufacturers to produce more goods in less time.

In 1846 Elias Howe invented the sewing machine. This machine allowed workers to produce clothing on a large scale. By 1860 factories in the Northeast produced at least two-thirds of the country's manufactured goods.

Transportation improvements helped new industries succeed. Thousands of miles of roads and canals were built between 1800 and 1850. Canals created new ways to ship goods by connecting lakes and rivers.

Technology and Industry (continued)

Contrasting

How did trade differ before and after the building of railways and canals?

_____

_____

_____

_____

Making Connections

Which of these inventions has largely replaced the telegraph? (Place a check mark next to all correct answers.)
- ❏ *telephone*
- ❏ *automobile*
- ❏ *computer*
- ❏ *television*

Traveling upstream became easier after Robert Fulton introduced a reliable steamboat in 1807. Steamboats could carry goods and people more cheaply and more quickly than flatboats and sailing vessels. Steamboats traveled the country's major rivers, canals, and the Great Lakes. This led to the growth of cities like Cincinnati, Buffalo, and Chicago.

Changes made to sailing ships also improved transportation. **Clipper ships** were ships with sleek hulls and tall sails. They could sail as fast as most steamships of the time.

Railroads also had a great impact on transportation. At first, short stretches of track connected mines and rivers. Horses pulled trains until steam locomotives were developed. In 1830 Peter Cooper built the first American steam locomotive, called the *Tom Thumb*. After improvements, steam locomotives began pulling trains in the United States. A railway network linking major cities grew throughout the country. A network of railroad track soon united the Midwest and the East.

Together, railways and canals changed trade. In the past, farm goods were shipped down the Mississippi River to New Orleans. From there, they were shipped to the East Coast or other countries. The railway system and east-west canals allowed products to be shipped directly from the Midwest to the East. Shipping was faster and cheaper, which made products less expensive. Railroads also made travel to Ohio, Indiana, and Illinois faster and more affordable, so the population of those states increased.

The growth of industry and travel created a need for faster methods of communication over long distances. An instrument called the **telegraph** filled that need. It used electric signals to transmit messages. The telegraph sent messages over great distances using **Morse code.** This code was created by American inventor Samuel Morse and used a series of dots and dashes to represent the letters of the alphabet.

Agriculture (pages 392–393)

Three key inventions of the 1830s changed farming methods and encouraged settlers to farm larger areas in the Midwest. The steel-tipped plow was invented by John Deere in 1837. It was much sturdier than wooden plows and could cut through prairie sod. The mechanical reaper, designed by Cyrus McCormick, sped up the harvesting of wheat. A third invention, the thresher, quickly separated the grain from the stalk.

Agriculture (continued)

Identifying

Name three inventions that improved farming in the 1830s.

1. _____

2. _____

3. _____

The new machines and railroads allowed farmers to grow more cash crops—crops raised strictly for sale. Midwestern farmers grew and shipped more wheat, and farmers in the Northeast and Middle Atlantic states grew more fruits and vegetables. The rocky soil of New England was poor for farming, but industry flourished there.

Section Wrap-Up

Answer these questions to check your understanding of the entire section.

1. **Analyzing** What innovation of the 1800s played a great role in the settlement of the Midwest? Explain your answer.

_____

_____

2. **Making Inferences** Why did industry thrive in New England instead of agriculture?

_____

_____

 **Persuasive Writing**

Samuel Morse had trouble convincing Congress to build a telegraph line. On a separate sheet of paper, write a letter that Morse could have used to persuade Congress.

The North's People

Essential Question

How did immigration have an impact on cities, industries, and culture in the North?

Directions: As you read, complete a graphic organizer like the one below to show how immigration affected the cities, industries, and culture in the North.

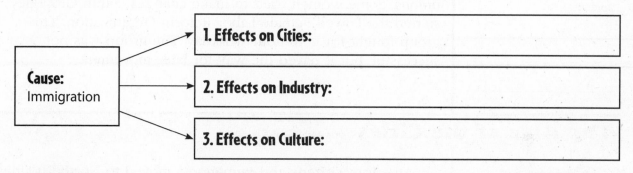

Cause: Immigration

1. Effects on Cities:

2. Effects on Industry:

3. Effects on Culture:

 **Notes**   **Read to Learn**

Northern Factories (pages 395–397)

Listing

Name at least three examples of poor conditions that existed in factories in the early 1800s.

1. _____

2. _____

3. _____

Many immigrants came to America for freedom. They lived in cities and worked in the mills and factories there. Working conditions were poor. Employees worked long days in dangerous conditions. Many adults and children were hurt. Factories were hot in the summer and cold in the winter. Factory owners were often more worried about profits than about the safety of workers, and there were no laws to protect workers.

By the 1830s, workers began to work together to improve conditions in the factories. They formed **trade unions.** A trade union is an organization of workers with the same trade or skill. In the mid-1830s, skilled workers in New York City held **strikes.** By refusing to work, they hoped to force employers to pay higher wages and to shorten their workdays. Going on strike was illegal at this time, so striking workers could be fired.

By the 1830s, slavery was uncommon in the North, but **prejudice** and **discrimination** still existed. Prejudice is an unfair opinion that is not based on facts. Discrimination is unfair treatment of a group. Few African Americans were allowed to vote. Most were not allowed to attend public schools and were forced to use separate schools and hospitals.

Northern Factories (continued)

Copyright © Glencoe/McGraw-Hill, a division of The McGraw-Hill Companies, Inc.

Making Connections

Define discrimination, and give an example of discrimination that exists today.

_____

_____

_____

Most African Americans were poor, but a few succeeded in business. Henry Boyd owned a furniture company in Cincinnati. Samuel Cornish and John B. Russwurm founded the first African American newspaper. Macon B. Allen was the first African American who was licensed to practice law.

Employers also discriminated against women workers. Women were paid less than men and were not allowed to join unions. Some women tried to make changes. Sarah G. Bagley started the Lowell Female Labor Reform Organization. This group fought for a 10-hour workday. The group was not successful, but it paved the way for later movements.

The Rise of the Cities (pages 397–399)

Drawing Conclusions

Check the best ending to the following statement.

Factory owners hired immigrants because
❏ *they wanted to learn from the immigrants' customs and languages.*
❏ *the immigrants brought experience and skill to the factories.*
❏ *the immigrants were willing to work for low wages.*

American citizens and immigrants moved to Northern cities to work in the factories. Employers welcomed immigrants because many of them were willing to work for low pay. Large cities grew even larger. Small villages located along rivers turned into major cities. St. Louis, Pittsburgh, Cincinnati, and Louisville became trade centers that linked farmers in the Midwest with cities in the Northeast. New cities like Buffalo, Detroit, Milwaukee, and Chicago grew along the Great Lakes.

Immigration to the United States greatly increased between 1840 and 1860. The largest group of immigrants came from Ireland. In the 1840s, most of the potato crops in Ireland were destroyed by a disease. This led to a **famine,** or an extreme shortage of food. As a result, many Irish men and women moved to America. They took low-paying factory jobs or worked on the railroads.

The second-largest group of immigrants came from Germany. Some came for work and opportunity. Others came because the democratic revolution in Germany had failed. Many were able to buy farms or open their own businesses.

Some people were opposed to immigration. They were known as **nativists**. They believed that immigration threatened the future of "natives," or American-born citizens. In the 1850s, they formed a new political party that became known as the Know-Nothing Party. This party wanted stricter citizenship laws. It also wanted to keep immigrants from holding office.

Answer these questions to check your understanding of the entire section.

1. **Specifying** Name three groups of people who were discriminated against in the early 1800s. Give a specific example of how each group was treated.

_____

_____

_____

_____

2. **Comparing and Contrasting** Explain the similarities and differences between the Irish and German immigrants.

_____

_____

_____

_____

On a separate sheet of paper, write an essay about the many ways that immigrants affected the character of the United States. Give specific examples to support your statements, but be sure to present your facts objectively without conveying opinions.

_____

_____

_____

_____

_____

_____

_____

_____

_____

_____

_____

_____

Southern Cotton Kingdom

Essential Question

How did the South's industry and economy differ from the industry and economy of the North?

Directions: As you read, complete a graphic organizer like the one below to show how the economies of the South and the North differed in the following areas.

```
          ┌──────────────────────────────────────────┐
          │  Differences Between the North and South  │
          └──────────────────────────────────────────┘
            │                    │                  │
  ┌──────────────┐    ┌──────────────┐    ┌──────────────────┐
  │ 1. Agriculture│    │ 2. Industry  │    │ 3. Transportation│
  │              │    │              │    │                  │
  │              │    │              │    │                  │
  └──────────────┘    └──────────────┘    └──────────────────┘
```

Notes

Read to Learn

Rise of the Cotton Kingdom (pages 401–402)

Analyzing

If the cotton gin made it possible for workers to clean cotton so much faster, why were more workers needed?

_____

_____

In the late 1700s, most people in the South lived along the Atlantic Coast in Maryland, Virginia, and North Carolina. This area was known as the Upper South. By 1850, the population of the South had spread inland to the Deep South. The Deep South included Georgia, South Carolina, Alabama, Mississippi, Louisiana, and Texas. The economy of the South was thriving, but it relied on slavery.

After the American Revolution, the demand for cotton from the South increased. But a lot of time and labor were needed to produce cotton. Workers had to carefully remove the sticky seeds from the cotton fibers by hand.

In 1793 Eli Whitney invented the **cotton gin.** This machine removed the seeds from cotton fibers. A worker could clean 50 times more cotton with the machine than by hand. Farmers began growing even more cotton to increase their profits. As a result, they needed more workers to plant and pick the cotton. The use of slave labor greatly increased because of this.

The Deep South grew mostly cotton, but rice and sugarcane were also grown. The Upper South grew tobacco, hemp, wheat, and vegetables. The Upper South also became a center for selling and moving enslaved people through the South.

 **Notes** | **Read to Learn**

Industry in the South *(pages 402–403)*

Why did cities in the South tend to grow more slowly than those in the North? (Check the correct answer below.)

❏ *Industry in the North was more profitable than agriculture in the South.*

❏ *Enslaved people did not want to live in big cities.*

❏ *There were fewer railroads in the South, and they were shorter and not linked to each other.*

The economy in the South became very different from the economy of the North. The South produced far fewer manufactured goods than the North. The South was slow to develop industry for several reasons. The first reason was the great increase in cotton sales. Growing cotton was very profitable. Second, people in the South had little **capital,** or money to invest in businesses. To build factories, planters would have had to sell land or enslaved people. Third, there was not a large market for manufactured goods in the South. Much of the population was enslaved people who could not afford to buy goods. Finally, many people in the South were happy with their profits from farming and did not want industry.

Some leaders of the South did want to increase industry in the region. William Gregg opened his own textile factory in South Carolina. Joseph Reid Anderson took over the Tredegar Iron Works in Virginia and made it into one of the country's top iron producers. The company provided weapons and other iron products during the Civil War. Leaders like Gregg and Anderson believed that the South depended too much on the North for manufactured goods. They also thought that factories would help improve the economy of the Upper South.

Most Southern towns were located on coasts or rivers. People in the South used natural waterways to ship goods. Roads in the South were poor, and there were few canals. The South had fewer railroads than the North. The railways in the South were short and were not linked to each other. For this reason, Southern cities grew more slowly than cities in the North. The lack of railways would hurt the South during the Civil War.

Section Wrap-Up

Answer these questions to check your understanding of the entire section.

1. **Analyzing** One reason that industry developed slowly in the South was the lack of capital to build factories. Why didn't planters sell their land or enslaved people to raise money for industry?

   _____

   _____

2. **Predicting** How do you think transportation and industry in the South would affect the region during the Civil War?

   _____

   _____

   _____

 **Expository Writing**

In the space provided, make a list of the pros and cons of developing industry in the South in the 1800s. Then use the list to explain whether more efforts should have been made to develop industry in the South.

_____

_____

_____

_____

_____

_____

_____

_____

_____

_____

_____

_____

The South's People

Essential Question

How did unique elements of culture develop among enslaved African Americans in the South?

Directions: As you read, fill in a graphic organizer like the one below to list and briefly describe the unique elements of culture that developed among enslaved African Americans in the South.

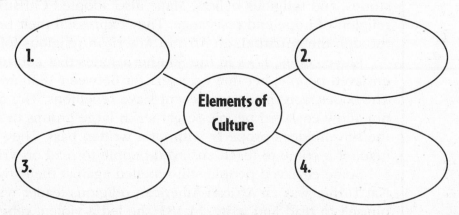

1.

2.

Elements of Culture

3.

4.

 **Notes**

Read to Learn

Farms and Plantations *(pages 407–408)*

Classifying

List the four categories of white Southerners from "wealthiest" (1) to "poorest" (4). Use what you have learned about land ownership and homes as a basis for your answer.

1. _____

2. _____

3. _____

4. _____

Most white Southerners fit into one of four groups. **Yeomen,** the largest group, were farmers who did not have enslaved workers. They grew crops for their own use and to trade with local merchants. The second group, **tenant farmers,** did not own their own land. Instead, they worked on landlords' estates and lived in simple homes. The third group, the rural poor, lived in crude cabins in wooded areas. They were proud of being self-sufficient. The last group was made up of plantation owners. A plantation could be as large as several thousand acres. Plantation owners measured their wealth by the number of enslaved workers they had.

Others were blacksmiths, carpenters, shoemakers, or weavers, but most enslaved African Americans were field hands. They worked from sunrise to sunset in the fields. They were supervised by an **overseer,** or a plantation manager.

Read to Learn

Life Under Slavery (pages 409–411)

Determining Cause and Effect

What was the effect of Nat Turner's rebellion?

_____

_____

_____

Enslaved African Americans suffered hardships and misery. They worked hard, earned no money, and had little hope of freedom. Yet they maintained their family life as best as they could and developed a culture of their own. They lived in constant fear of being separated from their families. This forced them to create large extended families. They held on to their African customs and passed on African music and dance, folk stories, and religious beliefs. Many also adopted Christianity as a religion of hope and resistance. They expressed their beliefs through the **spiritual,** an African American religious folk song.

Slave codes, laws in the Southern states that controlled enslaved people, became even stricter between 1830 and 1860. The codes were made to prevent slave rebellions. The codes did not allow enslaved people to gather in large groups or to leave the slaveholder's property without a written pass. They also made it a crime to teach enslaved people to read or write.

Some enslaved people still rebelled against their owners. Nat Turner was an African American religious leader who taught himself to read and write. In 1831 he led a violent rebellion in Virginia. His rebellion frightened white Southerners and led to stricter slave codes, but violent rebellions were rare. More often, enslaved people would rebel by working slowly or acting sick.

Some enslaved African Americans tried to run away to the North. Harriet Tubman and Frederick Douglass were two who succeeded. The Underground Railroad offered help to those who escaped. This was a network of "safe houses" owned by free blacks and whites who opposed slavery.

City Life and Education (page 412)

Making Inferences

Do you think that most Southerners valued education? Explain your answer.

_____

_____

_____

The South had several large cities by the mid-1800s. The 10 largest cities were seaports or river ports. Cities near the crossroads of the railways also began to grow. Whites, enslaved workers, and many free African Americans lived in the cities. Free African Americans were able to form their own communities in the cities. They practiced trades and founded churches and institutions, but their rights were limited.

No statewide public school systems existed at this time, but some of the larger cities opened public schools. The South was behind other parts of the country in **literacy,** or the number of people who are able to read and write. One reason for this was that people were more spread out in the South and could not send their children great distances to school. Many Southerners also believed that education was a private matter.

Answer these questions to check your understanding of the entire section.

1. **Diagramming** Complete the diagram below to indicate who supervised groups of workers on a plantation.

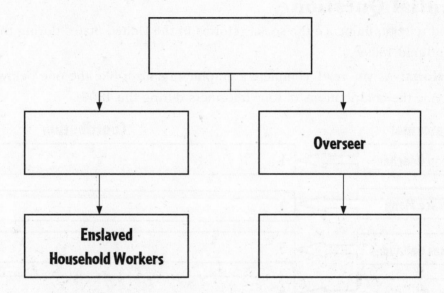

2. **Evaluating** What name was given to the laws in the Southern states that controlled enslaved people? Describe two of the laws, and tell how the laws were expected to prevent rebellions.

_____

_____

_____

_____

On a separate sheet of paper, write a short description of the life of an enslaved person. Use descriptive words that convey the information contained in your text and the content above.

Social Reform

Essential Question

How did religion influence the social reforms in the United States during the early and mid-1800s?

Directions: As you read, complete a graphic organizer like the one below to describe the contributions of four reformers during the 1800s.

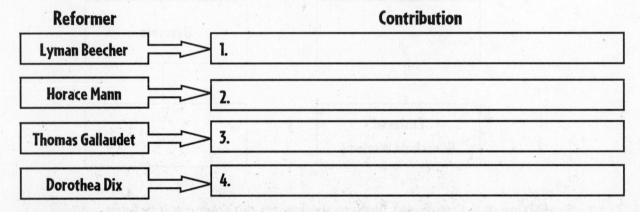

Reformer	Contribution
Lyman Beecher	1.
Horace Mann	2.
Thomas Gallaudet	3.
Dorothea Dix	4.

Notes

Read to Learn

Religion and Reform (pages 419–420)

Finding the Main Idea

Place a check mark next to the best statement of the main idea of this passage.

_____ *Several social reform movements started in the 1800s.*

_____ *Some reformers worked for temperance.*

Religious camp meetings, called **revivals,** were popular in the early 1800s. This was a time of religious fervor known as the Second Great Awakening.

This was also a time of reform in the nation. Some reformers wanted to improve society by setting up **utopias.** These were communities based on the idea of a perfect society. Most of these communities did not last.

Several social reform movements came about in the 1800s. Some reformers, like Lyman Beecher, called for **temperance.** This meant drinking little or no alcohol. These reformers used lectures and booklets to warn people about the dangers of liquor. The temperance movement led to the passage of some laws, but most of them were later repealed.

In the mid-1800s, most people did not believe in compulsory, or required, education. Education was also not available to girls or to many African Americans. Some reformers wanted to improve education. In Massachusetts, Horace Mann founded the nation's first state-supported **normal school.** This is a school in which people were trained to be teachers. Many colleges and universities were also set up during this time.

Religion and Reform (continued)

Listing

List three people who worked for reforms for people with disabilities.

1. _____

2. _____

3. _____

Some reforms helped people with disabilities. Thomas Gallaudet (GA•luh•DEHT) developed a way to teach people who could not hear. Samuel Gridley Howe helped teach people who could not see. He created books with large raised letters that people could "read" with their fingers. Dorothea Dix educated people about the poor conditions in which prisoners and mentally ill people lived.

Cultural Trends (page 421)

Identifying

Identify the person described in each of the following:

1. A transcendentalist who supported women's rights in her writings

_____

2. An American poet who wrote story poems

_____

3. Author of Uncle Tom's Cabin

_____

The changes in American society made an impact on art and literature. American artists started to develop their own style of art. Their art had to do with American themes.

The reform spirit had an effect on the **transcendentalists.** These thinkers and writers stressed the relationship between humans and nature. They also wrote about the importance of the individual conscience. The conscience deals mainly with a person's values or sense of right and wrong. In her writings, Margaret Fuller supported women's rights. She pushed for people to listen to their conscience and to rise above their prejudice. Henry David Thoreau practiced **civil disobedience.** He refused to obey laws he thought were unjust.

American poets also created great works. Henry Wadsworth Longfellow wrote story poems, such as the *Song of Hiawatha*. In *Leaves of Grass,* Walt Whitman captured the new American spirit. Emily Dickinson wrote personal poems.

Harriet Beecher Stowe wrote the best-selling novel in the mid-1800s. In her novel, *Uncle Tom's Cabin,* she wrote about the injustice of slavery.

Section Wrap-Up

Answer these questions to check your understanding of the entire section:

1. **Evaluating** Which reformer do you think made the most important contribution to American society? Why do you think so?

   _____

   _____

2. **Drawing Conclusions** How did art in the United States change in the 1800s?

   _____

   _____

Persuasive Writing

Take on the role of one of the reformers discussed in this section. In the space provided, write a letter to a friend persuading him or her to join the reform movement you represent. Include reasons why you think the reform movement is important.

_____

_____

_____

_____

_____

_____

_____

_____

_____

_____

_____

_____

_____

_____

_____

The Abolitionists

Essential Question

How did the abolitionists influence the antislavery movement?

Directions: As you read, complete a diagram like the one below to identify five abolitionists and their roles in the movement.

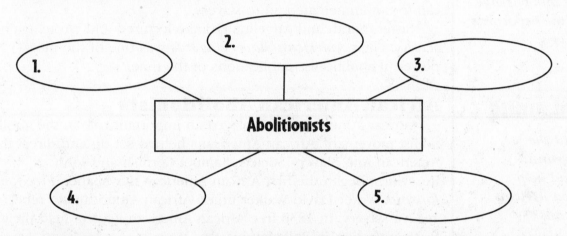

 Read to Learn

Early Efforts to End Slavery (pages 425–426)

Summarizing

What was the goal of the American Colonization Society?

_____

_____

_____

The spirit of reform in the early 1800s included the work of **abolitionists.** Abolitionists were reformers who worked to abolish, or end, slavery. Even before the American Revolution, some Americans worked to end slavery. By the early 1800s, slavery had ended in the Northern states. However, it was an important part of the South's economy. By the mid-1800s, many Americans came to believe that slavery was wrong. The conflict over slavery grew.

The first antislavery effort was not about ending slavery. Instead, its goal was to resettle African Americans in Africa or the Caribbean. The American Colonization Society was formed by a group of white Virginians. They freed enslaved people and sent them abroad to start new lives. Many were sent to Liberia in West Africa. The society had obtained land for a colony there.

The American Colonization Society did not stop the growth of slavery. The number of enslaved people kept growing, and the society could send only a small number of them to Africa. Besides, most African Americans did not want to go to Africa. Their families had lived in America for many years. They just wanted to be free.

Read to Learn

The Movement Changes (pages 426–430)

To identify the main idea of this passage, underline key words or phrases.

How did the Underground Railroad help enslaved African Americans?

_____

_____

_____

White Abolitionists

Around 1830, slavery became the most important issue for reformers. William Lloyd Garrison had a big impact on the anti-slavery movement. He started *The Liberator* and the American Anti Slavery Society. He was one of the first white abolitionists to call for an immediate end to slavery.

Sisters Sarah and Angelina Grimké lectured and wrote against slavery. Their *American Slavery As It Is* was one of the most powerful abolitionist publications of the time.

African American Abolitionists

African Americans also played an important role in the abolitionist movement. African Americans helped set up and direct the American Anti Slavery Society. Samuel Cornish and John Russwurm began the first African American newspaper, *Freedom's Journal*. Writer David Walker urged African Americans to rebel against slavery. In 1830 free African American leaders held their first convention in Philadelphia.

Frederick Douglass was the best-known African American abolitionist. He taught himself to read and write. Douglass escaped from slavery in Maryland in 1838. He settled in Massachusetts and then in New York. He was a powerful speaker who spoke at many meetings in the United States and abroad. Douglass was also the editor of the antislavery newspaper *North Star.*

Sojourner Truth escaped slavery in 1826. She worked with Frederick Douglass and William Lloyd Garrison to end slavery. She traveled throughout the North and spoke about her experiences as an enslaved person. She also worked in the women's rights movement.

Some abolitionists helped African Americans escape slavery. The network of escape routes from the South to the North was called the **Underground Railroad.** Along the routes, whites and African Americans guided the runaways to freedom in Northern states or Canada. Harriet Tubman became the most famous conductor on the Underground Railroad.

Clashes Over Abolitionism (pages 430–431)

Only a small number of Northerners were abolitionists. Many Northerners believed that freed African Americans could never blend into American society. Some Northerners were afraid that

Clashes Over Abolitionism *(continued)*

Listing

List two reasons Northerners gave for opposing abolition.

1._____

_____

_____

2._____

_____

_____

the abolitionists could begin a war between the North and South. Other Northerners feared that freed African Americans would take their jobs.

Opposition toward abolitionists turned cruel at times. Angry whites came into Elijah Lovejoy's antislavery newspaper offices and tore up his presses three times. The fourth time, the mob set fire to the building. When Lovejoy came out of the burning building, he was shot and killed.

Many Southerners said that abolitionism threatened the South's way of life. Southerners defended slavery. They thought it was necessary for the Southern economy. Southerners also said that they treated enslaved people well. Some defenses of slavery were based on racism. Many whites believed that African Americans could not take care of themselves and were better off under white care.

Section Wrap-Up

Answer these questions to check your understanding of the entire section.

1. **Drawing Conclusions** How did William Lloyd Garrison influence the abolition movement?

_____

_____

2. **Summarizing** Why were Southerners against abolitionism?

_____

_____

On a separate sheet of paper, write an article explaining the efforts of two abolitionists to end slavery.

The Women's Movement

Essential Question

What were the effects of the women's rights movement of the middle to late 1800s?

Directions: As you read, complete a graphic organizer like the one below to identify the contributions made by these three individuals to women's rights.

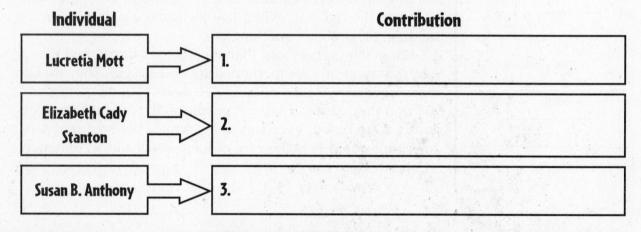

Individual	Contribution
Lucretia Mott	1.
Elizabeth Cady Stanton	2.
Susan B. Anthony	3.

Read to Learn

Women and Reform (pages 435–437)

Contrasting

Complete the following sentences: Elizabeth Stanton believed that suffrage

_____

_____.

Lucretia Mott believed that suffrage

_____

_____.

Many women abolitionists also worked for women's rights. In July 1848, Lucretia Mott and Elizabeth Cady Stanton set up the first women's rights convention in Seneca Falls, New York. The Seneca Falls Convention paved the way for the women's rights movement. The convention issued a declaration that called for an end to laws that discriminated against women. It called for women to be allowed to enter jobs and businesses that mostly men held.

An issue that created conflict at the convention was **suffrage**, or the right to vote. Elizabeth Stanton wanted the declaration to demand the right to vote for women. Lucretia Mott believed that women voting was too radical an idea. The convention decided to include the demand for woman suffrage in its declaration.

Susan B. Anthony also worked for women's rights. She called for equal pay for women, college training for girls, and coeducation. **Coeducation** is the teaching of males and females together. Anthony and Stanton joined together to win the right to vote for women. Women would not gain that right until 1920.

Progress by Women (pages 437–438)

Identifying

What barrier to women did Elizabeth Blackwell break?

_____

_____

_____

Some people called for better education for women. Catherine Beecher and Emma Hart Willard thought that women should be trained for their traditional roles in life. They also thought that women would make good teachers.

Some young women began to make their own opportunities. Emma Willard taught herself science and mathematics. She set up the Troy Female Seminary in New York. There, girls were taught math, history, geography, and physics, as well as homemaking subjects. Mary Lyon set up Mount Holyoke Female Seminary in Massachusetts.

In the 1800s, women made some gains in marriage and property laws. Some states began to recognize women's rights to own property after they married. Some states passed laws that allowed divorced women to share the custody of their children with their husbands. Some states also allowed women to get a divorce if their husbands abused alcohol.

In the 1800s, women had few career choices. Some professions, like medicine and the Christian ministry, were not open to women. Some women began to break through those barriers. Elizabeth Blackwell was accepted to a medical school in New York after being turned down several times. She graduated first in her class and became a famous doctor.

Section Wrap-Up

Answer these questions to check your understanding of the entire section.

1. **Summarizing** What demands were made at the Seneca Falls Convention in 1848?

   _____

   _____

   _____

2. **Synthesizing** What progress did women in the middle to late 1800s make regarding marriage and property laws?

   _____

   _____

   _____

Expository Writing

In the space provided, write a short essay about the efforts made by women in the 1800s to gain equal rights.

_____

_____

_____

_____

_____

_____

_____

_____

_____

_____

_____

_____

_____

Slavery and the West

Essential Question

Did the compromises made by Congress effectively address slavery and sectionalism?

Directions: As you read, complete a graphic organizer like the one below to identify how each of the following compromises addressed slavery.

Compromise	Major Ideas
Missouri Compromise (1820)	1. _____ 2. _____
Compromise of 1850	1. _____ 2. _____

Notes

Read to Learn

The Missouri Compromise (page 449)

Determining Cause and Effect

How would slavery in Missouri affect the balance of power and the laws about slavery?

_____

_____

_____

_____

_____

Many settlers who moved west to Missouri brought enslaved people with them. When Missouri applied for statehood, a debate began. In 1819, 11 states were free states, and 11 states were slave states. If Missouri entered as a slave state, then the balance of power in the Senate would change. There would be more senators from the slave states than from the free states.

Northerners and Southerners did not agree about slavery. Many Northerners wanted to ban it. Most Southerners did not like Northerners interfering in Southern business. These differences grew into sectionalism. **Sectionalism** is an exaggerated loyalty to a particular region of the country.

The Senate offered a solution to the problem. Missouri could enter the nation as a slave state, and Maine could enter as a free state. Henry Clay guided the Senate's bill through the House of Representatives. The House passed it by a close vote in 1820. The next year, Missouri became a state. This solution, known as the Missouri Compromise, kept the balance of power in the Senate.

A New Compromise (pages 450–451)

Copyright © Glencoe/McGraw-Hill, a division of The McGraw-Hill Companies, Inc.

Formulating Questions

Read the following words. Use these words in questions that could be answered by reading the text.

Free-Soil Party
fugitive
California

_____

_____

_____

_____

Identifying

Place a check mark next to the item that best completes the following sentence:

California entered the Union as a

❏ *free state.*

❏ *slave state.*

❏ *territory.*

The debate over slavery in new territories broke out once again. Texas became a state in 1845. Slavery was legal in Texas. The United States fought with Mexico and took New Mexico and California. Representative David Wilmot called for banning slavery in any lands taken from Mexico. This plan was known as the Wilmot Proviso. Southerners protested. They wanted the new lands to be open to slavery. Senator John C. Calhoun stated that Congress had no authority to ban slavery in any territory. No action on slavery was taken.

Both of the 1848 presidential candidates ignored the slavery issue. Their failure to take a stand made voters angry. Many of those who opposed slavery formed the Free-Soil Party. They selected a candidate for office, but he lost. Even so, the party gained some seats in Congress. Zachary Taylor won the election.

In 1849 California applied to become a free state. At the same time, antislavery forces wanted to ban slavery in Washington, D.C. Southerners, in turn, wanted a stronger **fugitive,** or runaway, law. They wanted runaways in the North to be returned to the South. However, the key issue was the balance of power in the Senate. If California entered as a free state, the slave states would be outvoted in Congress. They might not get their fugitive law passed. Angry Southerners talked about **seceding** from, or leaving, the Union.

Senator Henry Clay tried to find a way to solve the problem. California, Clay said, could enter the Union as a free state. The new territories would have no limits on slavery. The slave trade, but not slavery itself, would be banned in Washington, D.C. Clay also pressed for a stronger fugitive law.

Debate broke out in Congress. Some legislators favored Clay's plan. Others, among them President Taylor, opposed it. When Taylor died suddenly, Vice President Millard Fillmore took over. Fillmore favored Clay's plan.

The debate went on. Finally, to end it, Senator Stephen A. Douglas divided Clay's plan into parts that could be voted on separately. Several Whigs **abstained,** or did not vote, on the parts they opposed. Congress passed five bills in 1850. Taken together, these laws were called the Compromise of 1850.

Section Wrap-Up

Answer these questions to check your understanding of the entire section.

1. **Predicting** How might sectionalism affect the nation in the future?

   _____

   _____

2. **Analyzing** How did Clay's proposal for Washington, D.C., appeal to both the North and the South?

   _____

   _____

In the space below, write a campaign speech for the Free-Soil Party candidate in the 1848 election.

_____

_____

_____

_____

_____

_____

_____

_____

_____

_____

_____

_____

_____

_____

A Nation Dividing

Essential Question

How did popular sovereignty lead to violence in Kansas?

Directions: As you read, complete a graphic organizer like the one below to note reactions to the idea of popular sovereignty.

Popular Sovereignty

North

1. _____

2. _____

South

1. _____

2. _____

Notes

Read to Learn

The Fugitive Slave Act (page 453)

Classifying

Circle the statements below that are true.

Northerners obeyed the Fugitive Slave Act.

Southerners supported the Fugitive Slave Act.

Antislavery groups formed the Underground Railroad.

The Fugitive Slave Act set hundreds of enslaved people free.

Congress passed the Fugitive Slave Act in 1850. It was passed as an attempt to please slaveholders. The act required all citizens to help catch runaways. People who helped a fugitive avoid capture could be fined or sent to prison. Southerners thought this law would make Northerners understand and accept the rights of people in the South. Instead, the law turned more Northerners against what they saw as the evils of slavery.

After the act became law, slaveholders worked harder to catch runaways. They even tried capturing runaways who had been free and living in the North for years. The slaveholders sometimes took African Americans who were not trying to escape and forced them into slavery.

Some Northerners did not follow the Fugitive Slave Act. They felt it was wrong to help the slaveholders. Some Northerners spoke out against slavery. Others gave money to buy freedom for enslaved people. Still others helped runaways find their way to freedom through a network called the Underground Railroad. Northern juries often refused to convict those who were accused of breaking the Fugitive Slave Act.

Read to Learn

The Kansas-Nebraska Act *(pages 454–455)*

Sequencing

Circle the event that happened first.

Congress passed the Kansas-Nebraska Act.

Antislavery supporters form their own government in Kansas.

Charles Sumner is attacked in the Senate chamber.

Franklin Pierce is elected president.

Identifying

Which two groups were involved in a "civil war" in Kansas?

_____

_____

_____

Franklin Pierce became president in 1853. He planned to uphold the Fugitive Slave Act. The next year, Senator Stephen Douglas called for making the lands west of Missouri into two territories. These territories would be called Kansas and Nebraska. Douglas hoped that both North and South would like his plan to expand the nation.

Kansas and Nebraska's locations would make them free states. Douglas knew the South would object to adding free states. He then suggested that Congress not follow the Missouri Compromise. Instead, Douglas put forward the idea of letting the settlers in those areas vote on whether to allow slavery. He called this **popular sovereignty,** or allowing the people to decide.

Many Northerners did not approve of the plan. They were afraid that it would allow slavery in areas that had been free for more than 30 years. Southerners liked Douglas's idea. They believed that Kansas would be settled mostly by slaveholders. Douglas also had the backing of President Pierce. Congress passed the Kansas-Nebraska Act in 1854.

Right after the law passed, people rushed to Kansas. Thousands of pro-slavery supporters from Missouri crossed the border into Kansas just to vote in the election. They traveled in armed groups known as **border ruffians.** After the election, Kansas had a pro-slavery legislature.

The new Kansas legislature passed laws in favor of slavery. People who were against slavery refused to accept the laws. Instead, they armed themselves and had their own election. By 1856, Kansas had two rival governments.

In May 1856, fighting broke out between the two groups. Pro-slavery supporters attacked a town of antislavery supporters. The antislavery supporters fought back. John Brown, an abolitionist, led a group of people in an attack. His group killed five supporters of slavery. Armed bands of people soon roamed the area. The newspapers called the conflict the "Civil War in Kansas." A **civil war** is a conflict between people of the same country.

Fighting also broke out in Congress. Senator Charles Sumner spoke out against the pro-slavery forces in Kansas. He also criticized senators who favored slavery. A representative who was related to one of the senators took action. The representative entered the Senate chamber and attacked Sumner with a cane. These conflicts made tensions between the North and the South even worse.

Section Wrap-Up

Answer these questions to check your understanding of the entire section.

1. **Analyzing** How did Franklin Pierce's position on slavery affect the situation in Kansas?

_____

_____

2. **Hypothesizing** Why do you think popular sovereignty did not work in Kansas?

_____

_____

Descriptive Writing

In the space below, write a diary entry from the point of view of a Kansas settler. In the diary entry, describe the violence in Kansas and how it affected the people and government.

_____

_____

_____

_____

_____

_____

_____

_____

_____

_____

_____

_____

_____

_____

_____

_____

_____

Challenges to Slavery

Essential Question

What was the significance of the *Dred Scott* decision?

Directions: As you read, complete a graphic organizer like the one below to record events related to the *Dred Scott* case.

1. 1830s: _____ _____ _____	→	2. 1846: _____ _____ _____	→	3. 1857: _____ _____ _____

Notes

Read to Learn

A New Political Party (pages 457–458)

Naming

Which party, Republican or Democratic, was against slavery?

_____

_____

Other events drove the North and South farther apart. The Democratic Party began to divide, with many Northern Democrats leaving it. In 1854 antislavery Whigs and Democrats joined with the Free-Soilers to create the Republican Party. The Republicans did not agree with the pro-slavery Democrats and Whigs. Northerners liked the Republicans' message, and the party won seats in Congress. Most Southerners agreed with the Democratic candidates.

The Republicans chose John C. Frémont as their candidate for president in 1856. The Democrats chose James Buchanan. Another party, the Know-Nothings, also chose a candidate—former president Millard Fillmore. Buchanan won the election with 174 electoral votes. Frémont had 114 electoral votes; Fillmore received only 8 votes.

The *Dred Scott* Case (pages 458–459)

In the 1830s, a doctor from Missouri moved his household to Illinois, a free state. Dred Scott, an enslaved person, was part of this household. The doctor moved again to the Northwest

The *Dred Scott* Case (continued)

Locating

Underline in the text the Northerners' and Southerners' reactions to the Dred Scott *ruling.*

Territory, taking Scott with him. Later, after moving his family back to Missouri, the doctor died.

In 1846 Scott sued for his freedom. Scott said he should be free because he had lived in places where slavery was illegal. This case gained a lot of attention when it reached the U.S. Supreme Court in 1857. The Court ruled that Scott was not free, even though he had lived on free soil. The Court went even further and said that slaves were property. The Court also said that popular sovereignty and the Missouri Compromise were unconstitutional. Neither voters nor Congress could ban slavery. That would be like taking away a person's property.

The Court's decision divided the nation even further. Northerners were outraged. Southerners, on the other hand, were happy. They believed that nothing could now stop the spread of slavery.

Lincoln and Douglas (pages 460–461)

Finding the Main Idea

What is the main idea of the second paragraph?

_____

_____

_____

In 1858 the Senate election in Illinois drew national attention. Senator Stephen A. Douglas, a Democrat, was running against Abraham Lincoln, a Republican. Douglas was popular. Lincoln, on the other hand, was almost an unknown.

Lincoln challenged Douglas to several debates. The main topic of each debate was slavery. Douglas believed in popular sovereignty. He said that slavery could be limited if people voted against slaveholders' rights. Douglas accused Lincoln of wanting African Americans to have the same rights as whites. Lincoln denied this. However, he did say that African Americans had some rights and that slavery was wrong. Douglas won the election. But people liked Lincoln's clear thinking and the way he made his points in the debates. Lincoln became popular.

Southerners began to feel threatened by Republicans. In 1859 an act of violence added to their fears. The abolitionist John Brown led a group on a raid of Harpers Ferry, Virginia. Their target was an **arsenal,** a site where weapons are stored. Brown planned to give the weapons to enslaved African Americans for a revolt against slaveholders.

Local citizens and troops stopped the raid. Convicted of treason and murder, Brown was sentenced to death. His execution shook the North. Some antislavery groups did not approve of Brown's violent actions. Others saw Brown as a **martyr**—a person who dies for a great cause.

Section Wrap-Up

Answer these questions to check your understanding of the entire section.

1. **Evaluating** Do you agree with the Court's decision in the *Dred Scott* case? Explain your reasoning.

   _____

   _____

2. **Identifying Points of View** How did Douglas and Lincoln differ in their views about enslaved people?

   _____

   _____

In the space below, write a letter from the point of view of Dred Scott as he sits in the courtroom and hears the Court's ruling. Include vivid descriptions of the courtroom and describe how Dred Scott must be feeling as the ruling is read.

_____

_____

_____

_____

_____

_____

_____

_____

_____

_____

_____

_____

Secession and War

Essential Question

What role did the theory of states' rights play in the outbreak of the Civil War?

Directions: As you read, complete a graphic organizer like the one below
to list the first six states that joined South Carolina in seceding from the Union.

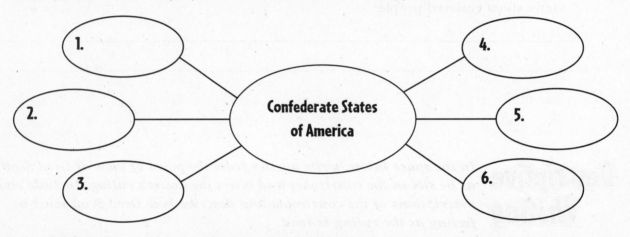

1.

2.

3.

Confederate States
of America

4.

5.

6.

Read to Learn

Secession (pages 463–465)

Identifying

Write the names of the presidential candidates for each party below.

1. Northern Democrats:

_____

2. Southern Democrats:

_____

3. Republicans:

_____

In the 1860 presidential election, Democrats were split over the slavery issue. Those in the North supported popular sovereignty. They chose Stephen Douglas as their candidate. Democrats in the South favored slavery and chose John Breckinridge.

Republicans chose Abraham Lincoln. The Republicans took the position that slavery should remain where it existed but not spread to territories. Lincoln won the election. The North outvoted the South. Lincoln's name was not on the ballot in most Southern states.

Republicans promised not to disturb slavery where it existed, but many Southerners did not trust them. On December 20, 1860, South Carolina left the Union. Other Southern states debated **secession,** or withdrawal from the Union. Congress tried to find a compromise to keep states from seceding. Senator John Crittenden called for amendments to the Constitution that would protect slavery. Republicans and Southern leaders did not accept this offer.

 **Notes** | # Read to Learn

Secession (continued)

Stating

Use the text to complete the following sentences:

1. The president of the Confederacy was

_____ .

2. The president of the United States was

_____ .

By February 1861, Texas, Louisiana, Mississippi, Alabama, Florida, and Georgia had also seceded. These states met with South Carolina leaders to form the Confederate States of America. They chose Jefferson Davis as their president.

Southerners in these states thought their decision to secede was right. They used the theory of **states' rights** to support their decision. They argued that the states had joined the Union of their own free will. They believed the Constitution was a contract among the independent states. The federal government had not honored that contract. As a result, they said, the states had a right to leave the Union.

Not all Southerners were happy with the decision to secede. Some Southerners did not believe in secession. Northerners also disagreed about secession. Some Northerners thought secession would be bad for the country. Others were glad to see Southern states leave the Union.

Lincoln asked the seceding states to rejoin the Union when he took office in March 1861. He pleaded for peace but told them that he would enforce federal law in the South.

Fort Sumter (page 466)

Speculating

Why do you think Lincoln sent an expedition with no weapons to Fort Sumter?

_____

_____

_____

_____

By the time Lincoln took office, Confederate forces had already taken some U.S. forts in their states. Lincoln did not want to start a war to take the forts back. He also could not let the Confederate states keep the forts. If he did, the seceding states might think they were right.

The day after Lincoln took office, the commander of Fort Sumter in South Carolina sent him a message. The fort was low on supplies, and the Confederacy wanted the fort to surrender. Lincoln decided to send an unarmed expedition with supplies to the fort. He ordered his troops not to fire unless they were fired on first. Lincoln left the decision to start shooting up to the Confederates.

Jefferson Davis made a fateful choice. He ordered his troops to fire on the fort before the Union expedition arrived. On April 12, 1861, shots were fired on Fort Sumter. U.S. forces could not reach the fort in time, and the fort surrendered two days later.

President Lincoln made a call for troops. Volunteers signed up quickly. Meanwhile, four more Southern states joined the Confederacy. The Civil War had begun.

Answer these questions to check your understanding of the entire section.

1. **Summarizing** Summarize the theory of states' rights.

_____

_____

_____

2. **Hypothesizing** In your opinion, why did Lincoln think it was important to keep the Union together?

_____

_____

_____

 **In the space below, write a message from President Lincoln to Jefferson Davis. Try to persuade Davis to call off the attack on Fort Sumter and rejoin the Union.**

_____

_____

_____

_____

_____

_____

_____

_____

_____

_____

_____

_____

_____

_____

The Two Sides

Essential Question
What were the strengths and weaknesses of the North and South?

Directions: As you read, complete a graphic organizer like the one below to list the strengths of the North and South.

North

South

1. _____
2. _____
3. _____

1. _____
2. _____
3. _____

 **Notes**

Read to Learn

Goals and Strategies *(pages 475–477)*

Identifying

Name the four border states.

1. _____
   _____
2. _____
   _____
3. _____
   _____
4. _____
   _____

Choosing sides in the Civil War was hard for the **border states** of Delaware, Maryland, Kentucky, and Missouri. Slavery was legal in all four states, but few enslaved people lived in them. The states had ties to both the North and the South. All four states had strategic locations that made them important to the Union. Abraham Lincoln worked hard to keep the four border states in the Union. Still, many people in those states supported the Confederacy.

The two sides in the Civil War had different advantages. The North had a larger population and better resources. The South had great military leaders and a strong will to fight. Confederate soldiers knew the land where most of the battles were fought and had a strong desire to defend it.

The two sides also had different goals. The South wanted to make itself an independent nation. It did not need to invade the North, but only needed to fight long enough to convince the North to give up. The North wanted to restore the Union. This meant invading the South.

The South hoped to get support from Britain and France because both countries depended on Southern cotton. The

Goals and Strategies (continued)

Defining

Define the terms below:

1. blockade:

_____

_____

2. export:

_____

_____

Southern strategy was to defend the South and hold on to as much territory as possible. Southerners believed Northerners would soon tire of the war.

The Union strategy had three main parts. First, the Union would **blockade,** or close, Southern ports. This would keep supplies from reaching the Confederacy. It would also keep the Confederacy from **exporting,** or selling, its cotton to other countries. Second, the Union planned to gain control of the Mississippi River. This would split the Confederacy in two and cut supply lines in the South. This plan was called the Anaconda Plan, after the snake that squeezes its prey to death. Third, the North planned to capture Richmond, Virginia, the Confederate capital.

Americans Against Americans (pages 477–479)

Describing

Highlight adjectives and descriptive phrases in the text that describe the life of a soldier in the Union or Confederate army.

The Civil War pitted friends and family members against one another. People enlisted for a variety of reasons. Some felt loyalty to their region or nation. Others worried they would be called cowards if they did not enlist. Still others went in search of excitement. Many teenage boys ran away from home and lied about their age to join the military. At least half of the soldiers in both the North and the South came from farms. At first, African Americans were not allowed in either the Confederate or the Union army. The Union changed this policy later in the war.

Both sides hoped for an easy victory when the war began. However, the war lasted far longer than most people thought it would. As a result, soldiers' terms became longer. By the end of the war, about 900,000 men fought for the Confederacy and about 2.1 million men fought for the Union.

Soldiers suffered terribly during the war. Camp life was often boring and uncomfortable. New rifles used during the war resulted in terrible losses on both sides. Faced with the horror of war, many soldiers deserted. One of every 11 Union soldiers and one of every eight Confederates ran away.

Section Wrap-Up

Answer these questions to check your understanding of the entire section.

1. **Assessing** How did the goals of the North and the South determine their strategies?

_____

_____

_____

2. **Summarizing** What were the three parts of the Union strategy for the war?

_____

_____

_____

Descriptive Writing

In the space below, write a letter home from a soldier in either the Confederate or the Union army. Use information you have read and your imagination to include descriptive details about camp life, battles, the soldier's sense of purpose, and other feelings.

_____

_____

_____

_____

_____

_____

_____

_____

_____

_____

_____

Early Stages of the War

Essential Question

Why did neither the Union nor the Confederacy gain a strong advantage during the early years of the war?

Directions: As you read, complete a graphic organizer like the one below to list three major battles in each section of the country and which side won each battle.

West

1. _____
2. _____
3. _____

East

1. _____
2. _____
3. _____

Notes

Read to Learn

War on Land and Sea *(pages 481–484)*

Determining Cause and Effect

Why did Union forces attack Fort Henry and Fort Donelson?

_____

_____

_____

Evaluating

In the text to the right, highlight the battle that gave the Union control of the Mississippi.

The first major battle of the Civil War took place on July 21, 1861. Union and Confederate forces met in northern Virginia at the Battle of Bull Run. At first, Union forces drove the Confederates back. Then the Confederate forces rallied under "Stonewall" Jackson, and Union forces retreated in a panic. Northerners were shocked by the defeat. They began to understand that the war could be long and costly.

The Union goal in the West was to gain control of the Mississippi River and its **tributaries,** the smaller rivers that flow into a larger river. This would cut Southern supply lines and allow Union ships and troops to move into the South. In early 1862, Union forces under Andrew Foote and Ulysses S. Grant captured Fort Henry on the Tennessee River and Fort Donelson on the Cumberland River.

In April some of the bloodiest fighting of the war took place at the Battle of Shiloh in Tennessee. The Union won, but both sides suffered huge **casualties,** or people killed or wounded. After Shiloh, Union forces captured Corinth, Mississippi, and Memphis, Tennessee. The North also won an important victory when the Union navy captured New Orleans on April 25, 1862. The South could no longer use the river to ship its goods to sea.

War on Land and Sea (continued)

Other battles were also taking place at sea. On March 8, 1862, the Confederacy's **ironclad** ship, the *Merrimack,* attacked Union ships off the coast of Virginia. The Union's ironclad ship, the *Monitor,* rushed toward Virginia. The two ironclads met in a historic battle on March 9. Neither side won.

War in the East (pages 484–486)

Identifying

Highlight the battles won by the Union in one color. Highlight the battles won by the Confederacy in another.

Who won more battles in the East?

Union forces were also trying to capture Richmond, Virginia, the capital of the Confederacy. Richmond was vulnerable to attack because it was close to the border with the Union. But Confederate armies were committed to defending it at all costs, and they kept it from falling until the end of the war.

The Confederate victories in the East were due mainly to the leadership of Generals Robert E. Lee and Stonewall Jackson. Both men knew the terrain, were able to move their armies quickly, and inspired their troops. In 1862 the Confederacy won the Seven Days' Battle, the Second Battle of Bull Run, and the Battle of Fredericksburg. Lee's army defeated a Union army twice its size at Chancellorsville in May 1863.

Lee's attempts to invade the Union failed, however. In 1862 Lee invaded Maryland and split his army into four parts. He hoped to confuse Union General George B. McClellan. Instead, two Union soldiers found a copy of the Confederate plan. This gave the Union an advantage. The two sides met on September 17, 1862. The Battle of Antietam was the deadliest single day of fighting of the war. It was an important victory for the Union. It forced Lee's forces to retreat back into Virginia.

The Emancipation Proclamation (pages 486–487)

President Lincoln hated slavery, but he did not want to make the Civil War a conflict to end it. He worried that many Union supporters would oppose ending slavery, especially those in the border states.

Abolitionists like Frederick Douglass urged Lincoln to make the war a fight to end slavery. Abolitionists argued that slavery was morally wrong. They also believed slavery was the root of the divisions between North and South. They pointed out that Britain and France might be less willing to support the South if the Union made the war a fight for freedom.

Read to Learn

The Emancipation Proclamation (continued)

Describing

What did the Emancipation Proclamation do?

_____

_____

_____

On September 22, 1862, Lincoln announced that he would issue the Emancipation Proclamation. This decree said that all enslaved people in the Confederacy were free on January 1, 1863. But the decree did not actually free anyone. It only applied to enslaved people in Confederate territory. The Union had no power to enforce the policy. Still, the proclamation had an important impact. It showed the world that slavery would be banned if the Union won the war.

Section Wrap-Up

Answer these questions to check your understanding of the entire section.

1. **Activating Prior Knowledge** How did the Battle of New Orleans fit into the Anaconda Plan?

_____

_____

2. **Making Inferences** Why do you think Confederate forces were victorious in the East but not in the West?

_____

_____

**Persuasive Writing**

On a separate sheet of paper, write an essay arguing why you think Lincoln decided to emancipate enslaved people in 1862 when he had not done so at the beginning of the war.

Life During the War

Essential Question

What social, political, and economic changes resulted from the war?

Directions: As you read, complete a graphic organizer like the one below. In the outer ovals, list how the economies of the North and the South were affected by the war. Where the ovals overlap, write what was true about the economies of both regions.

North   **South**

1.   3.   2.

 Notes   Read to Learn

A Different Way of Life (page 491)

Calculating

About how many children did not attend school during the Civil War?

_____

During the Civil War, life in both the North and the South changed dramatically. About half of the 12 million school-age children did not go to school. Some schools were closed because they were too close to battle sites or because they were used as hospitals. Many children worked to help support their families.

Parts of the South in the paths of the armies were destroyed. Many people had to flee their homes. The South also faced severe shortages of food and supplies.

New Roles for Women (pages 492–493)

Women in both the North and the South took on new roles during the war. They kept farms and businesses running. They served as teachers and clerks. They often had to make do with little money.

Women also served in the war. For the first time, thousands of women served as nurses. Dorothea Dix convinced officials to

New Roles for Women (continued)

Listing

List three new roles that women filled during the war.

1. _____

2. _____

3. _____

let women serve, and she recruited many nurses. Mary Edwards Walker was the first woman army surgeon. Clara Barton and Sally Tompkins cared for wounded soldiers. Some women served as spies. Others disguised themselves as men and became soldiers.

Prison Camps and Field Hospitals (pages 493–494)

Identifying

Underline the location of the Confederate prison camp. Circle the location of the Union prison camp.

Early in the war, the North and the South simply exchanged prisoners. When officials realized that the exchanged prisoners were returning to fight, they set up prison camps. Prisoners usually had only a blanket and a cup. Andersonville prison in Georgia was severely overcrowded. The prisoners lived in filthy conditions and received little to eat. Thousands of Union prisoners held there died from disease. At the Union prison in Elmira, New York, Confederate prisoners suffered from the cold and filthy conditions. A quarter of the prisoners held there died.

Wounded soldiers were treated in field hospitals near the battlefield. Disease struck often because troops were crowded together and drank from unsanitary water supplies. Some regiments lost half their men to disease.

Political and Economic Change (pages 494–497)

Defining

Define the vocabulary words below:

1. *habeas corpus:*

_____

_____

_____

2. *draft:*

_____

_____

_____

Both the North and the South faced rebellions. Food shortages in the South led to bread riots in Richmond, Virginia, and other cities. In the North, the War Democrats criticized how the Lincoln administration was running the war. Peace Democrats wanted the war to end immediately. They were nicknamed the Copperheads, because many people viewed them as dangerous traitors.

Habeas corpus was suspended in both regions. Habeas corpus is a legal protection against unlawful imprisonment. Thousands of Northerners who spoke out against the war were jailed without trial. Confederate President Jefferson Davis upset many supporters when he suspended habeas corpus.

Soon both sides had trouble recruiting enough soldiers. The Confederate Congress passed a **draft** law in 1862. A draft orders people to serve in the military during a war. In the North, the

Political and Economic Change (continued)

3. bounty:

_____

_____

_____

Determining Cause and Effect

Why did the New York City mobs turn against African Americans?

_____

_____

_____

Union offered a **bounty**, or a sum of money paid to encourage volunteers. Then, in March 1863, the Union also passed a draft law. In both the North and the South, a man could avoid the draft by paying a fee or hiring a substitute.

The draft law caused protests. Riots occurred in several Northern cities. In July 1863, mobs rioted in New York City. The mobs turned against African Americans because many workers had opposed the Emancipation Proclamation. They were afraid that freed blacks would take their jobs. More than 100 people died.

The war strained the economies of both sides, but the North was better able to cope with the costs of the war. Both governments sold war bonds, imposed new taxes, and printed money. Northern money was called **greenbacks.**

Northern industries made money by producing war supplies. Farms also profited from the war. But prices rose faster than wages because goods were in high demand. This general increase in prices is called **inflation.** Inflation was much worse in the South. War destroyed transportation systems and farms there. This severely limited the supply of food and other goods in the South.

Section Wrap-Up

Answer these questions to check your understanding of the entire section.

1. **Determining Cause and Effect** Why did many school-age children not attend school during the Civil War?

_____

_____

2. **Inferring** What do you think was the greatest danger for soldiers during the Civil War? Explain your answer.

_____

_____

Descriptive Writing

On a separate sheet of paper, write a letter from a prisoner of war to a family member living in your hometown. The letter should describe conditions in the camp using information from the text. Add details from your imagination.

Chapter 16, Section 3

The Strain of War

Essential Question

How did the events at Gettysburg and Vicksburg change the course of the war?

Directions: As you read, complete a graphic organizer like the one below showing the results and significance of the battles of Gettysburg and Vicksburg.

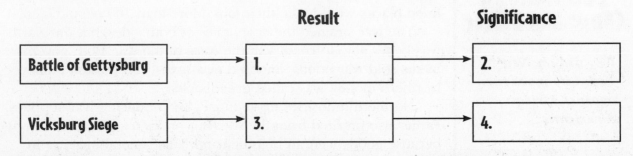

	Result	Significance
Battle of Gettysburg	1.	2.
Vicksburg Siege	3.	4.

Read to Learn

Southern Victories (pages 499–500)

Explaining

What was Lee's strategy at the Battle of Chancellorsville?

_____

_____

_____

_____

After Antietam, the Confederacy won a series of victories in the East because of the leadership of Generals Robert E. Lee and Stonewall Jackson. The Union commander, General Ambrose Burnside, began to march toward the Confederate capital at Richmond, Virginia. Lee moved his forces to Fredericksburg, where they dug trenches and waited for the Union troops. Lee's **entrenched** forces defeated Burnside's troops at the Battle of Fredericksburg. Burnside resigned.

Lee also had a brilliant strategy at the Battle of Chancellorsville. He divided his troops into three groups. One group stayed to defend Fredericksburg. Another group confronted the main Union force, now led by General Joseph Hooker, at Chancellorsville. A third group, led by Stonewall Jackson, attacked the Union forces in the rear. Confederate forces won the battle, but Jackson was wounded and later died.

These Confederate victories showed the weaknesses of the Union generals. General McClellan was reluctant to do battle. He did not obey Lincoln's order to follow the Confederate troops after the Union's victory at Antietam. Burnside was defeated at Fredericksburg, and Hooker was crushed at Chancellorsville. Within two months, Hooker had resigned as well.

Notes | Read to Learn

African Americans in the War *(page 501)*

Describing

Highlight adjectives and phrases that describe what African Americans faced in the military in one color. In another color, highlight phrases that describe African American soldiers' conduct in war.

African Americans were never allowed to enlist in the Confederate army. Confederate officials believed that African Americans might attack their fellow troops or begin a revolt if they were armed.

At the start of the war, the Union army also did not allow African Americans to enlist. Lincoln feared that allowing them to do so would anger people in the border states. By 1862, the North needed more soldiers. Congress allowed African Americans to enlist in all-black regiments. By the end of the war, African Americans made up about 10 percent of the Union army. They faced prejudice from other soldiers. They also faced fierce gunfire from Southern troops, who hated them. Nevertheless, they fought bravely and well. For example, the 54th Massachusetts served in the front lines of a battle to take Fort Wagner in South Carolina. The regiment suffered nearly 300 casualties. Their sacrifice made the 54th famous for its courage.

The Tide of War Turns *(pages 502–505)*

Sequencing

Number the following events in the order they occurred, from 1 to 4.

____ Pickett's Charge

____ Union victories split the Confederacy in two

____ Union and Confederate troops begin fighting in Gettysburg

____ Grant lays siege to Vicksburg

After the Confederate victory at Chancellorsville, Lee decided to invade the North. He hoped victories there would convince Britain and France to help the Confederacy. On July 1, 1863, his forces entered Gettysburg, Pennsylvania, searching for supplies. There, the forces met Union troops. On the first day of fighting, Union troops were outnumbered and retreated to a high section of ground called Cemetery Ridge. On the second day, Southern troops tried to force the Union troops from hills named Round Top and Little Round Top. On the third day, Lee ordered an all-out attack. Thousands of Confederate troops, led by General George Pickett, attacked Union forces on Cemetery Ridge. Three-quarters of those in Pickett's Charge were wounded or killed. On July 4, Lee retreated. The loss put an end to the Confederate hope of winning support from Britain and France.

The Confederacy lost other critical battles in 1863. In April of that year, Ulysses S. Grant had laid **siege** to Vicksburg, Mississippi. A siege means surrounding a place to keep it from receiving food or supplies. Both sides suffered heavy casualties. Vicksburg finally fell on the same day Lee retreated from Gettysburg. The Confederacy lost its last stronghold on the Mississippi River a few days later. The Union had cut off Arkansas, Louisiana, and Texas from the rest of the Confederacy.

 **Notes** |

The Tide of War Turns (continued)

On November 19, 1863, Soldiers' National Cemetery was dedicated at Gettysburg. The former governor of Massachusetts, Edward Everett, first gave a two-hour speech. Then President Lincoln rose and spoke for two minutes. His powerful words became known as the Gettysburg Address.

Section Wrap-Up

Answer these questions to check your understanding of the entire section.

1. **Evaluating** Which Union general proved to be the most capable? Explain your answer.

_____

_____

2. **Summarizing** What was the result of Pickett's Charge?

_____

_____

 **Expository Writing**

On a separate sheet of paper, write an essay comparing and contrasting the policies of the North and the South toward the enlistment of African Americans. Also discuss the treatment African Americans faced in the military.

The War's Final Stages

Essential Question

What events led to the end of the war?

Directions: As you read, complete a graphic organizer like the one below
to list the main components of Grant's total war on the South that led to the
end of the war.

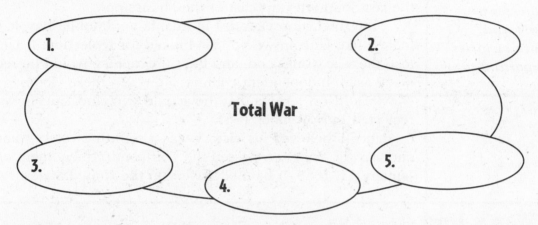

1.

2.

Total War

3.

4.

5.

Read to Learn

Total War Strikes the South *(pages 507–509)*

Making Inferences

*In the space below,
explain why Grant
pursued the strategy
of total war.*

_____

_____

_____

_____

By 1864, Union forces surrounded the South, blocking its
ports and controlling the Mississippi River. This cut off supplies
to the South. In March 1864, Lincoln put General Ulysses S. Grant
in charge of all Union armies. Grant's strategy was to deliver
killing blows from all sides. His armies would march to
Richmond, Virginia, the Confederate capital. At the same time,
Union General William Tecumseh Sherman would lead his troops
through the Deep South. This was a strategy of **total war.** Total
war is systematic destruction of an entire land, not just its army.

Grant led his army into the South. In May and June of 1864,
a series of three battles began in dense woods near Richmond
called the Wilderness. These battles were the six bloodiest
weeks of the war. The Union lost 50,000 troops in 30 days, but
Grant continued to fight. He moved his troops to Petersburg,
Virginia. This city was a Confederate railroad center that moved
troops and supplies. Confederate troops in the city held out for
nine months.

Read to Learn

Total War Strikes the South (continued)

Determining Importance

Underline the sentence to the right that expresses why Sherman's and Farragut's victories were important to the Union.

In July Sherman laid siege to Atlanta. The Confederates put up major **resistance,** or opposition. They held the city for almost two months. On September 1, Confederate forces finally abandoned the city.

In the meantime, David Farragut led a Navy fleet into Mobile Bay in Alabama. His action was a success and blocked the last Southern port east of the Mississippi.

Until the Union victories in Atlanta and Mobile Bay, it looked like Lincoln would lose his bid for reelection. If Lincoln lost, the war would end, and the Confederacy would be recognized as an independent country. However, these victories convinced Northerners that they could win, and Lincoln was reelected in November 1864.

Lincoln believed his victory was a sign that voters wanted to end slavery. Congress passed the Thirteenth Amendment on January 31, 1865. It banned slavery in the United States.

The War's End (pages 510–512)

Sequencing

Fill in the events in the time line below.

September 1, 1864:

_____

November 1864:

_____

April 2, 1865:

_____

April 9, 1865:

_____

The Union became even more determined to break the will of Southerners. Sherman's forces burned Atlanta and then marched across Georgia to the Atlantic coast. The troops tore up railroad lines, burned cities and fields, and killed livestock. This march became known as Sherman's March to the Sea. Sherman then continued through the Carolinas to join Grant's forces near Richmond. Thousands of African Americans fled their plantations to follow his army in a march to freedom.

On April 2, 1865, Petersburg finally fell to Grant's forces. Confederate leaders ordered weapons and bridges in Richmond burned and then fled the city. On April 9, Lee surrendered to Grant in Appomattox Court House, Virginia. Terms of the surrender were compassionate. The Union fed Confederate troops, and then they were allowed to make their way home peacefully.

The Civil War was the deadliest conflict in American history. Much of the South was destroyed, and it took years to rebuild. However, the North's victory saved the Union and freed millions of African Americans from slavery. The problems facing the nation would be addressed in the years following the Civil War. This period became known as Reconstruction.

Section Wrap-Up

Answer these questions to check your understanding of the entire section.

1. **Identifying** What did the Thirteenth Amendment do?

_____

_____

2. **Predicting** What were some potential problems that would have to be dealt with during Reconstruction?

_____

_____

_____

In the space below, write a letter from a soldier in Grant's army to his wife or parents at home on the eve of the third battle in the Wilderness. The letter should express what the soldier had experienced in previous battles as well as his feelings about the coming one.

_____

_____

_____

_____

_____

_____

_____

_____

_____

_____

_____

_____

_____

_____

_____

Chapter 17, Section 1 (Pages 518–521)
Reconstruction Plans

Essential Question

How did the plans to unify the nation differ after the Civil War?

Directions: As you read, complete a graphic organizer like the one below to show how the plans to reunify the country differed.

	Ten Percent Plan	Wade-Davis Plan	"Restoration"
Whose plan?	1.	1.	1.
Basic idea of plan	2.	2.	2.
Position on slavery	3.	3.	3.
Position on amnesty or allowing people to vote for delegates to the state conventions	4.	4.	4.
Position on Confederate leaders	5.	5.	5.

 **Notes**

Read to Learn

Reconstruction Debate (pages 519–520)

Drawing Conclusions

Why do you think Lincoln refused to offer amnesty to Confederate leaders?

_____

_____

_____

After the Civil War, the United States faced the challenge of reuniting and rebuilding the nation. Southern states had left the Union in 1861. They now needed to be readmitted. The economy and the society of the South also needed to be rebuilt. This period of rebuilding and readmitting the Southern states was called **Reconstruction.** Americans disagreed on the best way to carry out Reconstruction.

President Lincoln came up with the first plan to allow the Southern states back into the Union. His plan was known as the Ten Percent Plan. It said that a state could form a new government when 10 percent of the voters of the state took an oath to be loyal to the Union, The state must also adopt a new constitution that banned slavery. Lincoln wanted Southerners who supported the Union to take charge of the state governments. He did not want to punish the South. Lincoln offered Southerners **amnesty,** or a pardon, if they swore to be loyal to the Union. Confederate leaders were not included in this offer. In 1864 Louisiana, Arkansas, and Tennessee set up governments under this plan.

178

Chapter 17, Section 1

Reconstruction Debate (continued)

Making Inferences

Why did Radical Republicans deny seats to representatives from states that were readmitted under Lincoln's plan?

_____

_____

_____

_____

Some Republicans were less forgiving than Lincoln. Thaddeus Stevens and other Republicans wanted to put a more radical, or extreme, plan in place. They were called Radical Republicans. The Radical Republicans controlled Congress. They voted to deny seats to representatives from any state that was readmitted under Lincoln's plan.

In July 1864, Congress passed the Wade-Davis Bill. It said that a state must meet three requirements to rejoin the Union. First, a majority of the state's white males had to swear to be loyal to the Union. Next, only white males who swore that they had not fought against the Union could vote for delegates to a state constitutional convention. Third, any new state constitution had to ban slavery. The bill also said that former Confederates could not hold public office.

Lincoln would not sign the bill, but he wanted states to form new governments quickly. He knew that he would have to compromise with the Radical Republicans.

To help African Americans adjust to freedom, Lincoln and Congress set up the Freedmen's Bureau. It gave food, clothing, and medical services to African Americans. It helped them obtain land and find work for fair pay. It also set up schools.

Johnson's Plan (page 521)

Explaining

Why did John Wilkes Booth shoot President Lincoln?

_____

_____

On April 14, 1865, President Lincoln attended a play at Ford's Theater in Washington, D.C. During the play, John Wilkes Booth, an actor and Confederate sympathizer, shot and killed the president. The news shook the nation. African Americans and Northern whites mourned Lincoln's death.

Vice President Andrew Johnson became president. He had his own plan for Reconstruction, called "Restoration." It would grant amnesty to most Southerners when they swore loyalty to the Union. High-ranking Confederates could be pardoned only by the president. Johnson wanted to punish leaders whom he thought had tricked Southerners into seceding. His plan allowed only loyal, pardoned whites to vote for delegates to the state constitutional conventions. States also had to ratify the Thirteenth Amendment, passed by Congress in 1865. This amendment banned slavery. By the end of 1865, all former Confederate states except Texas had new governments and were ready to reenter the Union.

Answer these questions to check your understanding of the entire section.

1. **Analyzing** Why were African Americans and Northern whites so sad to lose Lincoln as a president?

_____

_____

_____

_____

2. **Explaining** What was the purpose of the Freedmen's Bureau?

_____

_____

Informative Writing

In the space provided, describe the challenges that the American people faced in the years following the Civil War. Discuss at least three challenges, and write a well-developed paragraph about each.

_____

_____

_____

_____

_____

_____

_____

_____

_____

_____

_____

_____

_____

_____

Radicals in Control

Essential Question

What were the results of Radical Reconstruction?

Directions: As you read, complete a graphic organizer like one below to list the results of Radical Reconstruction.

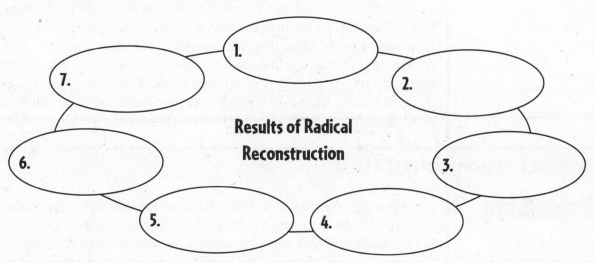

1.

2.

3.

4.

5.

6.

7.

Results of Radical Reconstruction

 **Notes**

Read to Learn

African Americans' Rights (pages 523–525)

Speculating

Why do you think riots broke out in the South? Check all that apply.

❏ *Blacks attacked white-owned buildings.*

❏ *Whites were angry about slavery ban.*

❏ *Whites opposed African Americans freedoms.*

❏ *Johnson vetoed the Civil Rights Act.*

In the fall of 1865, Southern states created new governments based on Johnson's Reconstruction plan. However, whites in the South burned churches, schools, and homes of African Americans. These riots convinced the Radical Republicans that Johnson's plan was too weak. When Southern representatives came to Washington, D.C., Congress would not seat them.

By early 1866, Southern states had passed **black codes.** These were laws to control freed men and women. They allowed plantation owners to take advantage of African American workers. The codes also allowed jobless African Americans to be arrested and fined. The codes banned African Americans from owning or renting farms.

Congress gave the Freedmen's Bureau the power to try people who violated the rights of African Americans. Congress then passed the Civil Rights Act of 1866. The act overturned the black codes and gave African Americans full citizenship. It also gave the federal government the right to step in to protect the rights of African Americans.

Read to Learn

African Americans' Rights (continued)

President Johnson vetoed the bills for the Civil Rights Act and the Freedmen's Bureau. But Republicans in Congress had enough votes to **override**, or defeat, both vetoes. The Radical Republicans knew at this point that they could not work with the president. They created a new Reconstruction plan of their own.

Congress passed the Fourteenth Amendment in 1866. It gave full citizenship to all people who were born in the United States. It included most African Americans but excluded Native Americans. The amendment also protected a citizen's life, liberty, and property. It barred Confederate leaders from holding national or state offices unless Congress had pardoned them. Southern states had to ratify this amendment to rejoin the Union.

Radical Reconstruction (pages 525–527)

Explaining

How were the Southern states run during the early part of Reconstruction?

_____

_____

After the elections of 1866, Radical Republicans controlled Congress. A period known as Radical Reconstruction began. Ten Southern states had not yet ratified the Fourteenth Amendment. The First Reconstruction Act required those states to create new governments. The act divided the 10 states into 5 districts run by military commanders until the states formed new governments. It barred Confederate leaders from office. It gave African American men the right to vote in state elections. The Second Reconstruction Act required the military commanders to register voters and prepare for state constitutional conventions.

Many white Southerners refused to vote in the elections for constitutional conventions and state governments. But thousands of African Americans did vote. This allowed Republicans to take control of the state governments. All 10 states rejoined the Union by 1870.

Johnson still had the power to direct the military commanders in the South. To limit his power, Congress passed the Tenure of Office Act. It said the president could not remove government officials without the Senate's approval. In 1867 Johnson removed Secretary of War Edwin Stanton from office without Senate approval. The House of Representatives voted to **impeach,** or formally charge, Johnson for his actions. But the Senate did not have enough votes to convict Johnson, and he remained in office until the next election.

Read to Learn

Radical Reconstruction (continued)

Identifying

What factors helped the Republicans win state elections in the South?

_____

_____

_____

In 1868 the Republicans backed Ulysses S. Grant for president. Grant won with the help of African American voters. In 1869 the Fifteenth Amendment was passed. It said that state and federal governments could not deny the right to vote to any male citizen because of race. It gave African American men the right to vote.

Section Wrap-Up

Answer these questions to check your understanding of the entire section.

1. **Determining Cause and Effect** Why did Congress write its own Reconstruction plan?

   _____

   _____

   _____

2. **Interpreting** What was the official reason for the impeachment of President Johnson by the House of Representatives? Could there have been underlying reasons as well? Explain your answer.

   _____

   _____

   _____

   _____

 **Descriptive Writing**

On a separate sheet of paper, write several paragraphs explaining how the Fourteenth Amendment affected the following groups: African Americans, Native Americans, and former Confederate leaders.

The South During Reconstruction

Essential Question

In what ways did government in the Southern states change during Reconstruction?

Directions: As you read, complete a graphic organizer like the one below to show the ways the governments in the Southern states changed during Reconstruction.

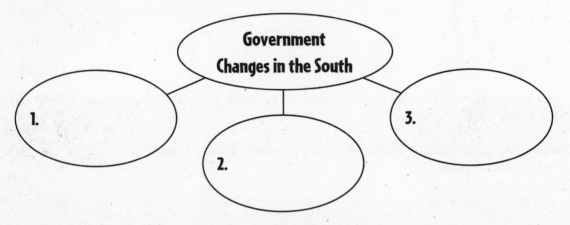

Government Changes in the South

1.

2.

3.

| Notes | Read to Learn |

Reconstruction Politics *(pages 529–530)*

Identifying

Name three groups that supported the Republican Party in the South.

_____

_____

_____

Republicans controlled Southern politics during Reconstruction. African Americans were an important part of Reconstruction politics. They were able to vote, and some became elected officials. Two African Americans, Hiram Revels and Blanche K. Bruce, became U.S. senators. Sixteen African Americans also served in the House of Representatives during this time.

Some Southern whites also supported the Republicans. Southern business leaders who supported the Union and non-slaveholding farmers were part of this group. Former Confederates called them **scalawags.** This meant "scoundrels" or "worthless rascals."

Some Northern whites moved to the South after the war. Many of these Northerners supported the Republicans as well. Southerners called them **carpetbaggers** because they used

Reconstruction Politics (continued)

Making Inferences

Why do you think members of the Ku Klux Klan wore white sheets?

_____

_____

cheap suitcases made from carpet fabric. Some carpetbaggers were dishonest, but many were reformers who wanted to help the South.

Many Southerners thought that the new Southern governments were corrupt, or dishonest. In reality, more **corruption** probably took place in the North than in the South.

Most white landowners in the South refused to rent land to freed African Americans. Store owners made them pay cash, and employers would not hire them.

The Ku Klux Klan and other secret organizations used fear and violence against African Americans. Klan members wore white sheets and hoods. They beat, wounded, and even killed African Americans and their white friends. They burned their churches, schools, and homes. Many planters, Democrats, and other Southerners supported the Klan. They saw violence as a way to control Republican power. In the early 1870s, Congress passed laws to stop Klan violence. But the laws did not have much success, because many Southerners would not testify against Klan members.

Education and Farming (page 531)

Describing

What challenges did African Americans in the South face as farmers?

_____

_____

_____

African Americans built their own schools during Reconstruction. The Freedmen's Bureau also supported education. Northern women and African Americans moved to the South to teach in the schools. Reconstruction governments built public schools for African Americans and whites. African American and white children usually went to different schools. Only a few states had laws that said schools must be **integrated.** Integrated schools are schools that have African American and white students. Most integration laws were not enforced.

Some African Americans were able to buy land with the help of the Freedmen's Bank. But most were not able to buy land. Many African Americans farmed using **sharecropping.** In the sharecropping system, a landowner rented a piece of land to a sharecropper, or farmer, along with a shack, some seed and tools, and sometimes a mule. The sharecropper would farm the land and pay the landowner a percentage of the crop.

Sharecroppers often had little left over after paying the landowners. Sometimes it was barely enough to feed their own families. Many felt that sharecropping was not much better than slavery.

Section Wrap-Up

Answer these questions to check your understanding of the entire section.

1. **Interpreting** How did most Southern whites view scalawags and carpetbaggers?

_____

_____

_____

2. **Theorizing** Why wouldn't most Southerners testify against Klan members?

_____

_____

_____

Expository Writing

In the space provided, describe the sharecropping system and explain why it was often viewed as another form of slavery.

_____

_____

_____

_____

_____

_____

_____

_____

_____

_____

_____

_____

_____

Change in the South

Essential Question

How did the South change politically, economically, and socially when Reconstruction ended?

Directions: As you read, complete a graphic organizer like the one below to show how Southern politics, the economy, and society changed when Reconstruction ended.

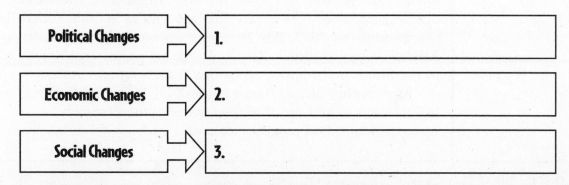

Political Changes	→	1.
Economic Changes	→	2.
Social Changes	→	3.

 **Notes** | **Read to Learn**

The End of Reconstruction (pages 535–537)

Determining Cause and Effect

What chain of events caused the economic depression of the 1870s?

_____

_____

_____

_____

Support for Reconstruction fell in the early 1870s. Northerners began to lose interest and wanted the South to take care of its own problems. Radical leaders lost elections or retired. Corruption in President Grant's administration and in Reconstruction governments spread. This caused some Republicans to leave the party. A group called the Liberal Republicans wanted to reconcile, or come together again, with Southern whites.

The Liberal Republicans helped pass the Amnesty Act. This act pardoned most former Confederates. It allowed nearly all white Southerners to vote and hold office again. Many of these people supported the Democratic Party. Democrats soon gained control of state governments in the South.

In 1873 poor railroad investments caused a major bank to close. A panic broke out. This forced smaller banks to close. It also caused a drastic drop in the stock market. Thousands of businesses shut down, and many workers lost their jobs. Republicans were blamed for the economic depression.

In 1874 Democrats gained seats in the Senate and won control of the House. This weakened support in Congress for

The End of Reconstruction (continued)

Reconstruction and African American rights. In the 1876 presidential election, the Democratic candidate, Samuel Tilden, appeared to be the winner. But some of the results were disputed, or questioned. Congress set up a special commission to review the election. The commission voted to give the election to Rutherford B. Hayes, the Republican candidate. Democrats threatened to fight the decision. Republican and Southern Democratic leaders met in secret. Hayes remained the winner, but an agreement was made. This agreement is often called the Compromise of 1877. The Democrats promised to maintain African American rights. The Republicans promised to give help to the South and remove all troops from Southern states.

After taking office, Hayes made it clear that the federal government would not interfere with Southern society. Reconstruction had come to an end.

Change in the South (pages 537–539)

Analyzing

What were the strengths and weaknesses of the South economically?

_____

_____

_____

When Reconstruction ended, new Democratic leaders took charge in the South. These Democrats called themselves "Redeemers." They lowered taxes and government spending. They also cut many social services that were started during Reconstruction.

The New South worked to develop strong industry. The area had coal, iron, tobacco, cotton, and lumber resources as well as a cheap and reliable workforce. Development of the railroad also helped industry in the South. The South made many advances in industry but did not develop an industrial economy as strong as the North's. Its economy still relied on agriculture.

The New South hoped to rely on small farms that raised a variety of crops instead of on large plantations that grew only cotton. But sharecropping and tenant farming increased, and these farmers grew **cash crops.** These are crops that can be sold for money. Cotton was the main cash crop. Too much cotton caused prices to fall. Sharecropping and relying on one crop hurt Southern agriculture.

A Divided Society (pages 539–540)

When Reconstruction ended, African Americans' rights suffered. African Americans had the right to vote, but state governments found ways around the Fifteenth Amendment. Many Southern states created a **poll tax.** This is a fee people

A Divided Society *(continued)*

Making Inferences

Could African Americans use the grandfather clause? Why or why not.

_____

_____

had to pay to vote. Many African Americans and poor whites could not afford the tax, so they could not vote. Some states made voters take **literacy tests.** In these tests, they had to read and explain parts of constitutions. Many African Americans could not pass the tests. Some whites could not pass the tests but were allowed to vote because of **grandfather clauses.** These laws allowed people to vote if their fathers or grand-fathers had voted before Reconstruction. Laws like these and the threat of violence caused fewer African Americans to vote.

Southern states also passed Jim Crow laws. These laws required races to be separated in almost every public place. In *Plessy* v. *Ferguson*, the Supreme Court ruled that **segregation,** or separation of the races, was legal as long as African Americans had access to public places that were equal to those of whites. In reality, public areas were separate but in no way equal.

Violence against African Americans increased. **Lynching** was one form of violence used. In a lynching, an angry mob killed a person by hanging.

Section Wrap-Up

Answer these questions to check your understanding of the entire section.

1. **Analyzing** Why were Democrats able to regain control of the state governments of the South?

_____

_____

2. **Interpreting** Who do you think gained more from the Compromise of 1877, Democrats or Republicans? Explain your answer.

_____

_____

**Descriptive Writing**

Assume you are an African American who lives in the South following Reconstruction. You want to vote at an upcoming election, but you are facing many challenges. On a separate sheet of paper, describe in detail the challenges that you face and how you feel about these challenges.